The
Philosophical & Theological Aspects
of
Interreligious Dialogue

Christian Heritage Rediscovered

The Series, as the name suggests, is meant to focus on Christian Faith & Living vis-à-vis topics like Literature & Poetry, Indigenous Philosophizing, Ethical response towards Agriculture, Health & Healing, Science & Technology, Ecofeminist Theology, Sociological approach towards Human Rights, Law & Politics, Arts, History of Ideas, Ancient Civilizations, Cultural Contiguity, Religious Cosmologies & Mysticism, Footsteps of famous Theologians, World Peace & Harmony, Global Capitalism, Network Marketing, Cybertheology, Population & Demographics, Epigraphic Studies, Contextualized Education, and many others. We welcome a Mss. on any topic/s mentioned, whether they are original works, scholarly monographs, collections of conference papers, revised dissertations, or translations of historical documents. Through the Series we, the Publishers, are striving to put forward published works that may help Institutions, Academic Bodies, Researchers, Scholars and the World at large in furthering their respective knowledge and understanding on the concerned subject. We welcome your comments on our efforts and further suggestions on how we can foster the upcoming thoughtful theologically grounded books.

Christian Heritage Rediscovered - 25

The Philosophical & Theological Aspects of Interreligious Dialogue

A Catholic Perspective

J. Kuruvachira

CWI

Christian World Imprints™

First Published in 2015 by

Christian World Imprints(TM)
Christian Publishing & Books from India
H-12 Bali Nagar, **New Delhi-110015**
info@christianworldimprints.com
www.ChristianWorldImprints.com
Phone: +91 11 25465925

ISBN 13: 978-93-5148-082-2 (HB) ISBN 13: 978-93-5148-096-9 (PB)

Cataloging in Publication Data--DK

Courtesy: D.K. Agencies (P) Ltd. <docinfo@dkagencies.com>

Kuruvachira, Jose, 1958- **author.**
The philosophical & theological aspects of interreligious dialogue : a Catholic perspective / J. Kuruvachira.
pages cm. -- (Christian heritage rediscovered ; 25)
Includes bibliographical references (pages) and index.
ISBN 9789351480822 (HB)
ISBN 9789351480969 (PB)

1. Christianity and other religions. 2. Religious pluralism--Catholic Church. 3. Catholic Church--Doctrines. 4. Catholic Church and philosophy. I. Title. II. Series: Christian heritage rediscovered ; 25.

DDC 261.2 23

Printed at D. K. Fine Art Press Pvt. Ltd.

The Book

This study presents the official teachings of the Catholic Church on interreligious dialogue as enshrined in the documents *Ecclesiam suam* (1964) of Pope Paul VI, *Nostra aetate* and other documents of the Second Vatican Council (1962-1965), *Dialogue and Mission* (1984), and *Dialogue and Proclamation* (1991), with some reflections on the philosophical and theological foundations of interreligious dialogue, and the present state of dialogue in the Catholic Church. The study can be used as resource material by students of Catholic theology, Catholic dialogue groups, and individuals involved in the practice of interreligious dialogue. It is also proposed to anyone who may be interested in knowing what the Catholic Church teaches about interreligious dialogue, be they non-Catholics, followers of other religions, or even non-believers.

The Author

J. Kuruvachira is Professor of Philosophy of Religion, History of Religions, and Interreligious Dialogue at the Salesian Pontifical University, Rome. He has a Doctorate in Philosophy from the Gregorian University, Rome, and a Master's degree in Roman Catholic Theology from Pavel Florensky School of Theology and Ministry, California (Euclid consortium).

Abbreviations

AA	*Apostolicam Actuositatem*
AAS	*Acta Apostolicae Sedis*
AG	*Ad Gentes*
c.	circa
CD	*Christus Dominus*
DH	*Dignitatis Humanae*
DV	*Dei Verbum*
EN	*Evangelii Nuntiandi*
GS	*Gaudium et Spes*
LG	*Lumen Gentium*
NA	*Nostra Aetate*
OT	*Optatam Totius*
PCID	Pontifical Council for Interreligious Dialogue
PO	*Presbyterorum Ordinis*
RH	*Redemptor Hominis*
RM	*Redemptoris Missio*
SC	*Sacrosanctum Concilium*

Introduction

Interreligious dialogue is a much discussed topic in our times, and its relevance is widely recognised not only by religious people but also by sociologists, historians of religions, psychologists, politicians and even diplomats. Interreligious dialogue is a practice that tries to build positive, co-operative and constructive interactions between followers of different religious traditions. Dialogue between religions is also becoming more are more indispensable for interreligious co-existence and promotion of peace in the world, and is envisaged as a way to find solutions to many of the conflicts in the world. Besides these pragmatic aims, from a philosophical and theological perspective, dialogue is seen as a common search for the truth. The Catholic Church, aware of these factors, has recognized the importance and necessity of interreligious dialogue, and considers it as one of the ways of carrying out her mission in the contemporary world.

This modest study aims at presenting the basic teachings of the Catholic Church on interreligious dialogue since the Second Vatican Council. It can be used as a resource material for students who do the basic course in Catholic theology where interreligious dialogue is generally part of the programme. It can be profitably utilised by any Catholic who wants to know what the Church teaches about interreligious dialogue. It is also offered to anyone interested in knowing about the teachings of the Catholic Church on interreligious dialogue, be they non-Catholics or non-Christians or even non-believers. In addition, it is proposed to students who pursue courses in history of religions, world religions, Catholic dialogue groups, and anyone who is involved in the practice of interreligious dialogue.

The first chapter attempts to provide some philosophical and theological reasons for interreligious dialogue. It tries to answer the question why one should engage at all in interreligious dialogue. Hence, an effort is made to present the existential, religious, metaphysical, epistemological, anthropological, ethical and cosmological reasons for interreligious dialogue. Besides, philosophy is considered as an indispensable help to deepen the understanding of theological issues – in the present case interreligious dialogue. The chapter also makes a brief presentation of some of the theological arguments for dialogue. The reason for placing together the philosophical and theological arguments in the same chapter is that, interreligious dialogue can be treated as an interdisciplinary subject inasmuch as it is relevant to both philosophy and theology.

The second chapter is an analysis of the teaching on dialogue in the encyclical letter of Pope Paul VI entitled *Ecclesiam suam* published in 1964 while the Second Vatican Council was in progress. He was the first to officially introduce dialogue into the life of the Catholic Church, and envisage it as the Church's proper answer to the signs of the times. Besides, it was this document that played the major role in inviting the Fathers of the Vatican II to consider dialogue as an art, style, spirit and method of the Church in the contemporary world. We can say, therefore, that, a doctrine of dialogue took shape in its essential principles with the publication of *Ecclesiam suam.* Hence, an acquaintance with the contents of this important document is indispensable for any discussion on interreligious dialogue.

The third chapter examines the teachings of the Declaration *Nostra aetate* of the Second Vatican Council which is considered as the 'charter of interreligious dialogue'. After analysing the contents of this document, the present study examines what the other documents of the Vatican II have to say about non-Christian religions, especially *Lumen gentium, Ad gentes, Gaudium et spes, Dignitatis humanae*, and others, so that one can get an overview of the teachings of the Vatican II on dialogue. Besides it was with the Second Vatican Council that the Catholic Church made the decisive option for interreligious dialogue as a method of carrying out her mission in the world.

The fourth chapter is an exposition of the contents of the document *Dialogue and Mission* issued by the Secretariat for Non-Christians in 1984. It is a text of considerable importance for understating the Catholic Church's view on interreligious dialogue during the early post-Conciliar period. The two major themes discussed in the document are the evangelising mission of the Church, and interreligious dialogue. It is meant as a help to Christians to encounter the followers of other religions, and a kind of support material for Christian communities, especially leaders, to live according to the directives of the Second Vatican Council.

The fifth chapter analyses the document *Dialogue and Proclamation* which was published on the occasion of the twenty-fifth anniversary of the Declaration *Nostra aetate.* It was a joint document of the Pontifical Council for Interreligious Dialogue (previously Secretariat for Non-Christians) and the Congregation for Evangelisation of Peoples, and was published in 1991. It attempts to explain that, interreligious dialogue and proclamation of the Gospel are two distinct elements of the *one* evangelizing mission of the Church, and wants to elaborate further on these two components of mission, and show how they are related to each other.

The sixth chapter is a brief examination of the state of interreligious dialogue today with reference to the functioning of the Pontifical Council for Interreligious Dialogue, practice of interreligious dialogue in local Churches, question of formation to dialogue, arguments against interreligious dialogue, a presentation of four major models of interreligious dialogue with a critical assessment of the merits and demerits of each, and the need to promote both interreligious dialogue and intercultural dialogue.

The documents analysed in this study manifest the growing awareness of the centrality of interreligious dialogue in the mission of the Church, and a development in her understanding of the same. The method followed in this study is expository, descriptive, analytical and critical. The author does not claim any real originality except perhaps in the first and sixth chapters and the sections in each chapter which contain the critical assessment of the document under investigation.

Today, most scholars and official documents prefer to use the concept 'other religions' instead of 'non-Christian religions'. Since both the terms are used in the ecclesial documents that we will be analysing in this study, we will also be using the same, and for us they mean one and the same reality.

The third chapter on *Nostra aetate* and the other documents of the Vatican II is a slightly improved version of the author's own article that was published with the title "Interreligious Dialogue in *Nostra aetate* and other Documents of Vatican II" in *Mission Today*, Vol. XVII, no. 1, January-March 2015, pp. 4-33. The fourth chapter is a reproduction, with minor changes, of another article published with the title "Interreligious Dialogue in the Document *Dialogue and Mission*" in *Mission Today*, Vol. XVI, no. 3, July-September 2014, pp. 196-220.

In the appendix the text of the Declaration *Nostra aetate* of the Second Vatican Council is reproduced. This being a fundamental document for any discussion on interreligious dialogue, a textual study of the same is highly recommended for the students of interreligious dialogue, and it is hoped that the insertion of this document in the appendix would facilitate it.

I am indebted to Professor Luis Roson Galache, the Dean of the Faculty of Philosophy, Salesian Pontifical University, Rome, for his help in getting this study published. I am also grateful to Professor Scaria Thuruthiyil and Professor Francis Vincent Anthony for reading the manuscript and making suggestions for improvement, to Antony Arulraj, New Delhi, India for doing the linguistic and stylistic corrections, and to Christian World Imprints for undertaking the publication of this book.

J. Kuruvachira
Rome
30 April 2015

Contents

Chapter 1

The Philosophical and Theological Foundations of Interreligious Dialogue

Most people today are familiar with the term 'interreligious dialogue', especially those who live in religiously pluralistic societies. In such cultural settings interreligious dialogue, in its multiple forms, is a fact of people's daily life, and is at the foundation of their social relations. As a reality, interreligious dialogue is not anything new in the history of religions. In fact, it is as old as religion itself, and it has been in practice since millennia, though the adherents of religious traditions may not have used the term 'interreligious dialogue'. Often dialogue contributed greatly to peaceful co-existence, friendship, solidarity, collaboration, mutual understanding and enrichment among the followers of various religions, and when it was neglected, their relationship was often marked by tensions, conflicts, violence, and even wars in the name of religion.

1. Meaning of interreligious dialogue

Dialogue is a two-way communication or a reciprocal conversation between two persons. As a form of communication it has a verbal connotation and implies the use of language. For human beings it is the fundamental and the most common form of communication and interaction. But in the field of religious relations, dialogue has a much wider connotation than mere verbal communication by two persons. It is a two-way communication between persons (or groups) who follow significantly different religious traditions. It implies various types of co-operative interaction among them for common good, and theological and spiritual exchange for mutual benefit. The dialogue can be carried out both at the individual level or at institutional level.

Interreligious dialogue consists of direct contact with people who belong to different religions, sharing of ideas, speaking and listening to each other, and working together for common good in an atmosphere of openness, friendship, equality and mutual respect, without fear or intimidation. It is a responsible way of relating with each other in order to discover the common elements in religions without eliminating or bracketing the essential differences among them. Dialogue aims at promoting understanding between religions, and the use of the potential of religious traditions for mutual enrichment and integral development of individuals and communities. When interreligious dialogue is between people of two religions it is called bilateral dialogue. When it is between people of more than two religions it is called multilateral dialogue.

Cardinal Jean Louis Tauran says that, interreligious dialogue is neither a mere conversation nor a diplomatic negotiation to find solution to a problem, but a pilgrimage and an adventure. It is a pilgrimage because one accepts to 'lose' time to look at the other and to listen to the other in order to understand who is he or she is, and in what he or she believes. It is an adventure because one asks the other who is his or her God, and how is his or her faith.[1] Dialogue

1 Cfr. Jean Louis Tauran, "Rendere ragione della propria speranza", in *Il dialogo interreligioso come fondamento della civiltà*, Enrico Bertoni (a cura di),

is not same as the study of different religions or comparative study of religions. It is neither a debate between followers of different religions nor is it same as ecumenical dialogue, nor is it an effort to persuade the other person to embrace one's own religion.[2] Dialogue does not believe in the power of force but in the power of reason and love. Dialogue is always between two real persons and not between two systems.

Interreligious dialogue is not just words or discussion only. Basically it is built upon human relationship. Dialogue can take place between individuals, groups and communities, and at various levels: for example, between neighbours, in schools, universities, work places, shopping centres, among academics and religious leaders. It can be formal or informal, bilateral or multilateral. Dialogue, therefore, is not just something that takes place on an official or academic level only, rather it is part of the daily life of people in which, led by a variety of motives, sometimes even out of necessity, the followers of different religions interact directly with each other as friends, helpers, well-wishers and collaborators.

But one cannot affirm with absolute certainly that all followers of religions are, by nature, inclined to constructive dialogue, communication and exchange with other religions. In all the major world religions there are certain right wing, conservative groups and organisations that are opposed to dialogue. Often their attitude towards other religions is marked by indifference, ignorance, suspicion, prejudice, domination, feeling of self-sufficiency, superiority, fanaticism, complacency, mutual fear, aggression and desire to impose their ideas on the others. This makes dialogue between religions problematic. As Catherine Corneille says, "[…] the main obstacle for dialogue lies not so much outside as within religious traditions."[3]

Milano, Maretti, 2009, pp. 74-75.

2 Cfr. Francis Arinze, *Meeting Other Believers*, Shillong, Vendrame Institute Publications, 1998, p. 4.

3 Catherine Corneille, *The Im-Possibility of Interreligious Dialogue*, New York, The Crossroad Publishing Company, 2008, p. 3.

2. Different terms used for interreligious dialogue

Sometimes different terms are used to refer to interreligious dialogue, such as, 'interfaith dialogue', 'interbelief dialogue', 'multifaith dialogue', etc. Though these terms can convey to a great extent what we generally mean by dialogue between followers of different religious traditions, following the official teaching of the Catholic Church, we retain the term 'interreligious dialogue'.[4] In fact, this is the term most commonly used in the official documents of the Catholic Church and in the magisterium of the Popes. The Vatican department for the promotion of interreligious dialogue is also named after this term: 'Pontifical Council for Interreligious Dialogue'.

3. Philosophical foundations of interreligious dialogue

One might ask: why should one engage in interreligious dialogue? Is it really necessary? What is the rationale behind promoting dialogue between religions? Are there philosophical and theological foundations for it? Below we shall try to answer these questions.

3.1 The existential fact of radical religious pluralism

Radical religious pluralism is an existential fact, and statistics of the religions of the world will easily confirm it. Every age has been a religiously pluralistic age from a global point of view. But for many centuries large portions of humanity were hardly aware of the existence of religious traditions different from their own. But today

4 Some have proposed the term 'interpath dialogue', instead of interreligious dialogue in order to avoid implicitly excluding atheists, agnostics, rational humanists, and others with no religious faith, but uphold certain ethical and human values, as well as those world religions that do not place the same emphasis on 'religious faith' as do some monotheistic religions such as Christianity, Judaism, and Islam. Another term in vogue is 'intercultural dialogue' where culture, and not religion, is the foundation for dialogue, and religion enters into this form of dialogue only inasmuch as it is considered as part of culture. Some have proposed the term 'transblief dialogue' in order to refer to those dialogues between rationalist groups that transcend all worldviews, whether religious or cultural or political. These three forms of dialogue go beyond the realm of religion proper, and therefore, they are not of relevance to us in the present context.

there is a growing awareness of the religious diversity of the world, and many envisage that it will remain as a permanent reality.

The religions are immense reserve of spirituality, interiority and positive values. In the history of religions we come across many living religions and numerous 'obsolete' ones; there are archaic religions and modern religions; there are major world religions and minor ones based on the number of adherents they have; there are 'ethnic' religions bound to specific cultures, and missionary religions with a universal appeal; there are traditional religions with less insistence on written sacred scriptures and systemically developed theology and philosophy, and those with highly developed doctrines and dogmas, and an immense variety of sacred scriptures; there are religious families with a common name but under its umbrella there are numerous denominations and sects; there are religions that vie with each other even to the degree of confrontation to win more followers for themselves, and there are those that grow only demographically with little or no interest in growth through missionary work. Since the World War II, all over the world, many cities have become multicultural and multi-religious, and people of different religions rub shoulders with each other far more than in the past. Religion also has a growing role in public life. In such a world of religious pluralism no religion can remain isolated. Today it is impossible for any religion to exist in splendid isolation and ignore the others. The belief that religious pluralism is not needed, and that a single religion is enough for all the peoples of the world is simply an utopia.

Most countries of the world have always been multi-religious. For example, Christianity was born in a religiously plural world, and throughout its history developed in that context. The same can be said of the religions of Egypt, Greece, China, India, Rome, and others. The religions of these civilizations did not take refuge in total isolation or lived in constant conflict with each other but they regularly interacted, exchanged ideas and entered into 'dialogue' with one another. In fact, most of the known religions of today are results of mutual fecundations. The overall tendency among them has been one of mutual acceptance, respect, toleration, co-operation and learning from one another, notwithstanding the differences, occasional conflicts and persecutions, rivalries and competitions, and attempts at eliminating religious minorities in order to create a mono religious culture.

But it is also to be stated that, in the past, among many religions, the desire to dialogue was not a dominant tendency. The religious quest was mainly directed towards the deepening of one's own religious belief, to defend it, and to preserve one's religious identity, and this naturally meant a certain degree of isolation from others. But today none can deny that there exists a growing desire for open dialogue with other religions. In most universities, Religious Studies, History of Religions, Theology of Religions and Philosophy of Religion are very attractive disciplines that draw many students. There is a natural curiosity among many people to get more information about the religion of the others. Among the thinking people of all religions there is a growing tendency to engage in systematic studies and researches on the doctrines, dogmas, beliefs, practices and sacred texts of the other. All this is due, not only because of the pressure of exterior events, such as, the present conflict between religions, but also on account of internal motives deriving from an intellectual dynamism to know more about the other. Thus, *radical religious pluralism serves as the existential context for interreligious dialogue.* In fact, it provides the necessary condition for it. Hans Küng says: "Genuine dialogue is possible only when there is a genuine plurality of theologies."[5]

3.2 Globalisation of religion

Globalisation can be described as a process of increased interrelationship and interdependence between the nations and cultures of the world. It is a process which transforms the world into a global market, not necessarily into a community of nations working closely together for peace, justice, harmony and civilizational growth, but into competitors and rivals. The powerful forces of globalization are affecting not only market forces and cultures, but also *religions.*

5 Hans Küng, *On Being Christian*, Edward Quinn (tr.), London, Xpress Reprints, 1995, p. 105.

With globalisation the old geographic religious boundaries have been blurred. Today, all major religions are found in all countries. The world has become a 'market' of religions in which everyone can pick and choose their religion, religious texts, religious practices, religious teachings and religious values. The mass media, travels, immigration, religious tourism, and the frequent encounters with followers of other religions in work places and centres of studies, have accelerated the process of globalization of religion. This has created, on the one hand, a new situation where interreligious dialogue is an unavoidable religious imperative and a historical duty, and on the other hand a new situation that challenges the traditional religious authorities, institutions, values and practices that were considered sacred and inviolable for centuries. This situation has also given rise to the emergence of religious fundamentalism and fanaticism, as means to defend one's religious identity, traditions, practices, and to overcome the uncertainty and insecurity created by a globalised world.[6] Thus, in an increasingly globalised world with multi-religious communities becoming more usual, it will become increasingly clear to all religions that, exclusivism is not a viable option, and that interreligious dialogue is an unavoidable obligation. Besides, today people are also speaking about the necessity of dialogue between religions in international diplomacy, an element that was often neglected in the past.[7] Consequently, in a *religiously globalised world, interreligious dialogue cannot anymore be considered as a marginal issue, but something that is necessary and indispensable.*

3.3 The ontological dynamism in religions for dialogue

Religion by its very nature has a built-in ontological dynamism for dialogue. The first reality that distinguishes a religion from all other groups and associations is that, it is primarily directed towards a

6 Cfr. Heredia Rudolf, "Religious Fundamentalism: Reaction and Response", *Vidyajyoti*, 68, January, 2004, 36.

7 For a detailed discussion on this theme see Douglas Johnston and Cynthia Sampson (eds.), *Religion, the Missing Dimension of Statecraft*, Oxford, Oxford University Press, 1994.

transcendent. In fact, the main function of religion is to help people to establish a relationship with the transcendent, and this already implies a going out of oneself to 'meet the transcendent other' in order to engage in a dialogue-relationship with it. Here, the kind of dialogue is in the *vertical* direction. If the transcendent is conceived as a person, as in theistic religions, the quality of dialogue is higher than those faiths where the transcendent is not conceived as such.

Religion not only implies a private, vertical dialogue with the transcendent, but also a dialogue in the *horizontal* direction with the members of a cult-group. A good religion by its very nature must create and sustain social relationship because the field of religion is one of personal relationship. Religion involves a communal, co-operative, and joint activity in religious matters. All these presuppose a constant internal dynamism to dialogue among the members of a religious group, and such a dialogue builds up and strengthens the bond of unity among them.

Most religions have much to do with *revelation*, and every revelation involves some form of dialogue. The recipient of revelation is not always passive. The subject responds to the content of revelation or to the one who reveals a religious truth in the form of doubt, interrogation, request for clarification and expression of various emotions as reactions to the revelation. All these can be considered as different elements and manifestations of dialogue.

In every religious person there is a frequent *inner conversation* going on with one's own self on matters of religious nature. It is a personal dialogue within oneself in the depth of one's being in the form of an intrapersonal soliloquy. It is an interior meeting with one's own self, an introspection into the richness of one's being, and a silent dialogue within oneself, which Pope Paul VI, by referring to Thomas Aquinas called it a kind of 'dialogue of intelligence' (*mentis colloquium*).[8] Such an inner dialogue can take the form of deep reflection, silence, questioning, use of gestures, symbols, comparison,

8 Cfr. *Insegnamenti di Paolo VI*, Vol. XII, Città del Vaticano, Tipografia Poliglotta Vaticana, 1974, pp. 1212, 1234.

and seeking answers to certain personal problems and those affecting of the world.

Religious persons and institutions have a *natural tendency* to engage in dialogue with followers of other religions. This can be out of curiosity to know what others believe, to compare and contrast their beliefs and practices with one's own, the desire to learn from others, or simply co-operate as religious persons for some practical ends.

Religions, in general, manifest a tendency to make their *religious message known to others* in order to win new followers. This is true even of those religions which are not strictly missionary in nature. Even if a religion is not missionary by nature, there is always a dialogue with the society outside it, where it necessarily encounters followers of other religions. Proclamation of a religious message to others also involves dialogue because it is always carried out in a dialogical spirit: a religious message is presented, people ask questions, clarify doubts, and there is mutual enrichment through sharing of religious knowledge and experiences, and all these belong to the realm of dialogue.

But it is also true that, a religious person or group can freely choose not to dialogue with others. The moment dialogue ceases and people live isolated from one another, a religious faith inevitably becomes identified with exclusive belief with all the negative results that history in general and the history of religions in particular have made so painfully familiar.[9] The refusal to dialogue leads to incomprehension, misunderstanding, intolerance, fanaticism, fundamentalism, violence, terrorism and even wars in the name of religion.

3.4 Anthropological foundations of dialogue

Dialogue expresses an essential aspect of the human spirit. Human beings by nature are *relational beings*, and the desire to enter into dialogue with others is innate in them. The dynamism to dialogue

9 Cfr. Raimon Panikkar, *The Intrareligious Dialogue*, New York, Paulist Press, 1978, p. 18.

with other religions is derived also from this anthropological foundation. Mere curiosity about what the other believes, desire to know the other, learn from the other in order to enrich oneself, co-operation in social life, feeing of inadequacy, promotion of peaceful co-existence, desire to avoid conflicts or resolve conflicts are among the anthropological foundations for interreligious dialogue.

Religion is not something that a person can dismiss as irrelevant for human life. Religion as openness to transcendence is shared by all peoples. In this sense, it is not the privilege of a few, but is common to all human beings of all cultures. Raimon Panikkar says that it is 'the primal anthropological act' which every person performs in one way or another.[10] Jean Danielou says: "An aptitude for religion is a human datum. It can exist alike among non-Christians as among Christians."[11] In this sense, the *religious dimension of the human person* serves as a basis for anthropological unity, and consequently also for dialogue between religions.

The *common humanity* shared by all human beings is also at the foundation of interreligious relations. The appeal to a common humanity is not merely because of a pragmatic desire to justify interreligious dialogue and co-operation between religious persons. The idea of a shared and interdependent humanity points to the distinctly personal basis of dialogue, in which, encounters for interreligious dialogue are not meetings between two or more religions in the abstract (for example Buddhism, Christianity, Hinduism, Islam or any other religion) but, rather, an encounter of human beings – of individual persons who profess a particular religious faith. Interreligious dialogue is, in fact, the movement from thinking and talking about 'religion in general' to thinking and talking in some way about what people believe and practice as human beings.

---

10 Cfr. Ibid., p. 21.

11 Jean Danielou, *God and the Ways of Knowing,* Walter Roberts (tr.), San Francisco, Ignatius Press, 1957, p. 10.

3.5 Cosmological foundations of dialogue

Every religion has a cosmic dimension because it cannot be outside it. The material dimension of religion confirms this fact (eg. sacred stones, sacred rivers, sacred mountains, sacred plants, sacred animals, sacred times and seasons, astronomy, astrology, religious edifices, statues, paintings, sacred books, concern with human body, etc). The entire cosmos is a network of relations and an interrelated entity. Scientists tell us that even the subatomic parts are interrelated. Relation implies some form of 'dialogue', and dialogue is at the foundation of any relation. There is a *silent cosmic dialogue of interrelationship going on ever since creation.* It is a complex, multilateral dialogue from which nothing is excluded. Human beings are part of the cosmos and so are also religions. Religions being part of the cosmos are a complex web of relations. Consequently they have a natural propensity to be open to dialogue and mutual interaction. The history of religions tells us that no religion came with absolutely new beliefs or practices which never existed before. Religions dialogued, interacted, borrowed and built upon things which were already existing and then added to them their fresh insights and new revelations. As one can verify from the history of religions, Christianity is built upon Judaism; Hinduism took ideas from the religion of Indus Valley Civilisation, Buddhism, Jainism and traditional religions of India; Buddhism borrowed ideas from Jainism and Brahmanism; Islam took ideas from Judaism, Christianity and Arabian traditional religions. Concepts such as contemplation, prayer, pilgrimage, sacrifice, sin, reward, priest, prophet, punishment, redemption, liberation and salvation are common to most religions and are also products of borrowing and lending. Thus in some way, every religion is a product of dialogue and interrelationship. No religion is a self-sufficient monad, and no religion can exist without some reference to other religions, just like nothing in the cosmos can exist without some reference to others. Hence, the *radical interrelationship that exists in cosmos* can provide a cosmological foundation for interreligious dialogue.

3.6 Epistemological foundations of dialogue

Search for the truth is the ultimate aim of interreligious dialogue. Pope Benedict XVI says that, the purpose of dialogue is search for the truth, and he calls it 'dialogue of truth'.[12] Impelled by nature, and by a moral obligation, all human beings are obliged to search for the truth, especially religious truth.[13] Religious truth, is not something that one possesses once and for all. The ultimate truth of religion is always a mystery, and it has to be constantly searched for and grasped. No one religion can claim that it is already in possession of the whole truth. Even if a religion claims that it possesses the whole truth, finite human beings cannot possess it fully in this life. For example, though Christianity claims that Jesus Christ is the fullness of truth, no Christian can say that he or she has possessed him fully and once and for all, because knowing Christ is a lifelong process. A similar thing can be said of knowing the truth about the Brahman of the Upanishads by a Hindu, the truth of Nirvana by a Buddhist, the truth of Yahweh by a Jew, the truth of Allah by a Muslim and so on.

When dialogue is envisaged as a possibility of learning from another religion, it becomes part of a continuous religious pursuit of truth. It consists of an open and constructive exchange between individuals belonging to different religions, oriented to the possibility of change and growth. This notion of dialogue may include not only verbal exchange, but also serious engagement with sacred texts and teachings of another religion, and may also focus on questions of doctrine, practice, or organisation.[14]

The value of dialogue between religions is precisely to help one perceive that there are other windows of truth and other perspectives of truth. Therefore, one needs the other in order to know and verify one's own perspective of the truth. Raimon Panikkar says that,

---

12 Cfr. *Insegnamenti di Benedetto XVI,* Vol. I, Vatican City, Libreria Editrice Vaticana, 2006, p. 306.

13 Cfr. *Insegnamenti di Benedetto XVI,* Vol. VII part 1, Vatican City, Libreria Editrice Vaticana, 2012, p. 540.

14 Cf. Catherine Corneille, *The Im-Possibility of Interreligious Dialogue*, p. 3.

interreligious dialogue is a preparation for and a stepping stone to the mystical adventure of seeking the truth from within more than one religious tradition.[15] Dialogue believes that it can arrive at the truth by relying on the subjective consistency of the dialogical partners. Hence, the *primary aim of dialogue is the common search for the truth* by trusting the other, in deep honesty and great intellectual openness.[16] In this way, dialogue becomes a common search for the truth, sharing of the truth one possesses with others, verifying the truth which one possesses, correction of errors, and adherence to the truth when discovered, and this may call for conversion of mind and heart, and even of change of one's religious affiliation.

3.7 Ethical foundations of dialogue

It has been suggested by Raimon Panikkar that, interreligious dialogue is an expression of one's love of neighbour. If one is asked to love one's neighbour as oneself (Mk 12:31), and this neighbour has another religion, one cannot love him or her if one forgets or belittles his or her religion.[17] Unfortunately, what one often comes across in interreligious relations is mutual suspicion, indifference, prejudice, exclusivism, ghetto mentality, ignorance, opposition, intolerance, denial of religious liberty, freedom of conscience and human rights. In these conditions no love of neighbour can be practiced in the true sense of the term. One way to remedy such a situation is active promotion of interreligious dialogue.

Pope Benedict XVI has argued that, religion, like science and technology, philosophy and all expressions of human search for truth can be corrupted. Religion is disfigured when pressed into the service of ignorance, prejudice, contempt, violence and abuse. In this case,

15 Cfr. Raimon Panikkar, *The Intrareligious Dialogue*, p. 52.

16 Cfr. Raimon Panikkar, *The Unknown Christ of Hinduism. Towards and Ecumenical Christophany*, Bangalore, Asian Trading Corporation, revised and enlarged edition, 1982, p. 35; Id., *Myth, Faith and Hermeneutics. Cross Cultural Studies*, Bangalore, Asian Trading Corporation, 1983, p. 243.

17 Cfr. Raffaele Luise, *Raimon Panikkar. Profeta del dopodomani*, Milano, San Paolo Edizioni, 2011, pp. 104, 108.

one sees not only a perversion of religion, but also a corruption of human freedom, a narrowing and blindness of the human mind.[18] There can also be ideological manipulation of religion for political ends, and this becomes catalyst for division and tension and even violence in society.[19] He also says that, religions can be abused for doing evil and become vehicles of hate and conflict, and by calling upon God, people can justify violence.[20]

The 21st century is marked by increasing incidents of religious conflicts, violence, rise of religious fundamentalism and fanaticism in which followers of many religions are involved, either directly or indirectly, as their perpetrators or as their victims. In some parts of the world, religion is used as a powerful means for mobilising people for secular objectives, notably the acquisition of political power. It is here that dialogue becomes a useful tool, though not the only one, to promote peace in the world.

Raimon Panikkar says that until recently peace was considered as a political question. But the vast majority of wars has had a clear religious connotation or at least given a religious justification or inspired by a religious ethos. Therefore, peace is eminently a religious question, and dialogue is a way to it.[21] Lee H. Hamilton says: "In the numerous conflicts of identity that are currently raging in such places as the Balkans, the Middle East, Africa, and South Asia, one invariably finds a religious dimension. While religion is clearly central to so much of the strife that is taking place, it is also being looked at as an instrument of peace."[22] In addition, realisation of justice,

---

18 Cfr. *Insegnamenti di Benedetto XVI,* Vol. V part 1, Vatican City, Libreria Editrice Vaticana, 2010, p. 757.

19 Cfr. Ibid., p. 761.

20 Cfr. *Insegnamenti di Benedetto XVI,* Vol. III part 2, Vatican City, Libreria Editrice Vaticana, 2008, p. 491.

21 Cfr. Raimon Panikkar, *Cultural Disarmament, The Way to Peace,* Robert R. Barr (tr.), Louisville, Westminster John Knox Press, 1995, pp. 29-33; Id., *Myth, Faith and Hermeneutics*, p. 232.

22 Lee H. Hamilton, "Foreword", in Douglas Johnston (ed.), *Faith-Based Diplomacy. Trumping Realpolitik*, Oxford, Oxford University Press, 2003, p. ix.

forgiveness, reconciliation, human dignity and freedom are founded on dialogue.[23]

Dialogue can help to free religion from being misused by political ideologies, as instrument for the promotion of narrow cultural nationalism, oppression of religious minorities and denial of human rights. When dialogue is practiced it can promote social harmony, national integration and peaceful co-existence between followers of different religions. Commitment to common social concern can also be a basis of dialogue between religions. Such a dialogue would mean that urgent human needs can be tackled together rather than separately. The need to promote good relationship among nations is another ethical reason to engage in interreligious dialogue. Hans Küng has argued that, no human existence is possible without a world ethic shared by the nations, no peace between nations can be conceived without peace among the religions, and no peace among the religions can be envisaged without dialogue among the religions.[24] Hence, it is clear that *there are solid ethical reasons for promoting interreligious dialogue.*

4. Theological foundations of interreligious dialogue

Interreligious dialogue has solid theological foundations.[25] Dialogue has a *Trinitarian foundation* in the Holy Trinity of the Father, the Son and the Holy Spirit, which is a community of persons in communion. From a Christian perspective, human beings created in the image and likeness of God, are called to share the divine life of communion of the Holy Trinity in this world, and this naturally calls

23 Cfr. Raimon Panikkar, *Cultural Disarmament*, pp. 23, 63-74, 100-103.

24 Cfr. Hans Küng, "Foreword to the Second Edition", in Hans Küng, Josef van Ess, Heinich von Stietencron, Heinz Bechert, *Christianity and World Religions. Paths of Dialogue with Islam, Hinduism, and Buddhism,* Peter Heinegg (tr.), New York, Orbis Books, 1993, p. xiii.

25 This is a very vast and complex field of theology of religions. Here we mention only the main points without going into details, and leave the elaboration of the same to the experts in theology of religions.

for dialogue. Besides, God is in constant dialogue with humanity since the beginning of human history.[26]

Dialogue has a *Christological foundation.* Jesus Christ through his incarnation began a visible and tangible dialogue with humanity. During his public life he was open to all peoples, cultures and religions. He entered into dialogue with gentiles and recognised the good that was in them. His invitation to enter into the Kingdom of God was not confined only to the chosen people but also to all peoples. Thus, the universal character of the mission of Jesus went beyond the lost sheep of Israel, and manifested an open attitude towards all peoples. As sharers of the mission of Christ, Christians are to continue this dialogue initiated by Christ.

There is a *penumatological foundation* for interreligious dialogue. The Holy Spirit is present and at work in the world since creation. His presence is all pervading which does not exclude other religions. Wherever elements of truth are present, the Spirit is already there, and in all religions there are sparks of the divine truth.

The Church is the universal sacrament of salvation, and is meant for all men and women till the end of the world. Even if some people do not accept faith in Christ and baptism into the Church, the Church is to be an agent that fosters justice, reconciliation, unity and love among all human beings, not only among the circle of those who call themselves Christian, but also with all others, and this presupposes dialogue. Besides, the Church is not separated from the world, but part of it. Dialogue is also part of the Christian mission in the world. In fact, dialogue is an element of the evangelising mission of the Church, and one of its expressions.[27] These arguments can provide an *ecclesiological foundation* for interreligious dialogue.

Dialogue has an *anthropological foundation.* The common origin and the common destiny of all human beings, is another theological reason for entering into dialogue with followers of other religions. The Biblical tradition teaches that, the entire human race shares a

26 Cfr. *Dei verbum* in *Acta Apostolicae Sedis,* 58 (1966), no. 3.

27 Cfr. John Paul II, *Redemptoris Missio,* in *Acta Apostolicae Sedis,* 83 (1991), no. 55.

common origin and a common destiny in God. This human and spiritual unity in the origin and destiny of human beings, impels them to seek a common path in the quest for the fundamental values of life. Thus, as men and women of religion, all are challenged by the widespread longing for justice, peace, equality, freedom, human rights, development, solidarity, security, defence of life, protection of the environment and the resources of the earth. This is because religious people too have a specific contribution to offer in the search for proper solutions to these pressing questions, while respecting the legitimate autonomy of temporal affairs. It is here that interreligious dialogue becomes a useful tool to bring people together and work to find solutions to these problems that affect all, irrespective of religion.

The reason for dialogue is also based on the *theology of revelation*. Once many Christians thought that, the non-Christian religions would disappear as Christianity spreads all over the world. Now they know that perhaps they are here to stay, and have a role to play in God's plan. It is acknowledged that God can speak to human beings also through non-Christian religions. Jean Danielou says: "The first sign of the meeting between God and man is that of the pagan religions."[28] Besides, there are also great religious geniuses outside Christendom.[29] Christians are therefore required to search for and discover what might be revealed in these religions because the non-Christian religions also play a role, even if mysteriously, for the coming of the Kingdom of God. Hence non-Christian religions are not accidents or mere human creations. They too are part of God's saving plan for human beings. From the Christian point of view, they are *praeparatio evangelica* ('preparation for the Gospel'). In this sense, they have a value of their own, and a right to exist, and consequently, dialogue with them is indispensable.

All this would mean that, Christianity has to face the challenge of encounter with non-Christian religions. Plurality of religions is not an evil which needs to be removed but rather a wealth which is

28 Jean Danielou, *God and the Ways of Knowing*, p. 9.

29 Cfr. Ibid., p. 30.

to be welcomed and enjoyed by all. If the Spirit of God is at work in the entire universe, he is also at work in non-Christian religions inasmuch as they are bearers of things that are true, good and noble, and capable of making human beings better and serve as foundation for sound culture. When the positive elements of religions are lived meaningfully, they can humanise the world. Besides, religions also, in some way, enable people to work out their salvation, to be in contact with the transcendent, and live a virtuous life on this earth. All these are sufficient reasons for Christians to enter into dialogue with the followers of other religions.

When one speaks of interreligious dialogue, some of the questions that can naturally arise in the minds of people are: what is the need for it? Why is there so much insistence on interreligious dialogue today? Has not Christianity survived, grown and expanded for centuries without it? The answer is that, as we have already said above, interreligious dialogue is a practice as old as religion itself, and religious people have always dialogued with one another (and also quarrelled with each other), and dialogue is going on even now at different levels and with different degrees of success. But since the Second Vatican Council, there is a new consciousness in the Church of the need for a formal and institutionally supported dialogue with other religions. Today world religions are confronting each other as never before, and one can be truly religious only through interreligious relations. Hence, the insistence of the Catholic Church on interreligious dialogue is to be interpreted as an aspect of the *development of doctrine in the Church* in response to the signs of the times. God's action in history is continuous, and it is part of God's pedagogy to teach and instruct his people according to their mental and cultural development, and in response to new situations and conditions. Cardinal John Henry Newman says that, if Christianity is a universal religion, suited not simply to one locality or period, but to all times and places, it cannot but vary in its relations and dealings towards the world around it, that is, it will develope.[30] Hence, one

30 Cfr. John Henry Newman, *An Essay on the Development of Christian Doctrine*, Notre Dame, University of Notre Dame Press, [1878], 6th edition, 1989, p. 58.

can rightly say that, the new teaching of the Catholic Church on interreligious dialogue is a typical expression of the development of doctrine.

5. Conclusion

There are many philosophical and theological reasons for engaging in interreligious dialogue. These reasons are closely related to each other, and have to be taken in their entirety, in order to give a solid foundation for promoting interreligious dialogue. Dialogue is an ontological need of human beings, cultures, societies, religions, and nations. Today, in a globalised world, religious people are forced to be religious 'interreligously'. One cannot anymore walk alone as a religious person. Interreligious dialogue is a sign that other religions are to be recognised, accepted, taken seriously, respected and listened to. Interreligious dialogue is not just something that takes place at the academic or institutional level only. It is also part of the daily life of people and a way of life, and belongs to a culture of living together by interacting with one another as good neighbours, friends and acquaintances who mean each other's wellbeing and common good. When relationship between religions is seen in this perspective, interreligious dialogue can greatly contribute to the promotion of justice, peace, human rights, mutual enrichment and to civilizational growth. This is the reason why the Catholic Church insists with all the baptised, and all people of good will, to involve themselves actively in interreligious dialogue, which is an important aspect of the mission of the Church, and of a civilised way of life.

Chapter 2

Dialogue in the Encyclical *Ecclesiam Suam* of Pope Paul VI

The pontificate of Pope Paul VI (Giovanni Battista Montini),[1] lasting fifteen years (1963-1978), is assessed by historians as one of the most important in the history of the Catholic Church in modern times. He is considered as an intellectual of wide culture with great openness and pastoral progressivism. The three appellations attributed to him, namely, 'Pope of Vatican II', 'Pope of Dialogue' and 'Pope of Peace' sum up, to a great extent, the major directions in his apostolic ministry as the bishop of Rome. He is credited with the first title because, at the death of Pope John XXIII on 3 June 1963, he re-convoked the Second Vatican Council, gave it priority and direction,

1 Giovanni Battista Montini (1897-1978) was elected Pope on 21 June 1963, at the death of Pope John XXIII (1881-1963), and chose the name 'Paul VI'. He died on 6 August 1978. The diocesan process for his beatification and canonisation began on 11 May 1993. On 20 December 2012 he was declared venerable by Pope Benedict XVI. On 19 October 2014 he was beatified by Pope Francis.

and brought it to a successful conclusion in 1965; the second, because his pontificate was characterised by efforts at promotion of dialogue with all categories of people and the world at large; and the third, due to his untiring efforts at promoting world peace. He wrote seven encyclicals[2] and ten apostolic exhortations.[3] This chapter is a brief examination of his views on dialogue as enshrined in his encyclical *Ecclesiam suam* ('His Church', 6 August 1964) with some critical comments.[4]

1. Paul VI as a Pope of dialogue

Pope Paul VI was the first to officially introduce dialogue into the life of the Catholic Church and envisage it as the Church's proper answer to the signs of the times. His first encyclical *Ecclesiam suam* is called by some as 'the *magna charta* ('great charter') of dialogue'.[5] It describes Church's dialogue as a 'continuation of God's dialogue with the human race', and as a 'dialogue of salvation'.[6] He affirmed that, dialogue requires a method and institutional structures for promoting

2 They are: *Ecclesiam Suam* (1964); *Mense Maio* (1965); *Mysterium Fidei* (1965); *Christi Matri* (1966); *Populorum Progressio* (1967); *Sacerdotalis Caelibatus* (1967); *Humanae Vitae* (1968).

3 They are: *Signum Magnum* (1967); *Petrum et Paulum Apostolos* (1967); *Recurrens Mensis October* (1969); *Quinqueiam Anni* (1970); *Evangelica Testificatio* (1971); *Octogesima Adveniens* (1971); *Marialis Cultus* (1974); *Nobis in Animo* (1974); *Paterna cum Benevolentia* (1974); *Evangelii Nuntiandi* (1975).

4 It is to be clearly stated at the start that, *Ecclesiam suam* does not exhaust the teachings of Pope Paul VI on dialogue. In order to have a more complete view of his magisterium on this topic, one needs to study all his encyclicals, apostolic exhortations, homilies, discourses, interviews, etc. In this chapter we will limit ourselves to the contents of the encyclical in question with occasional references to other relevant sources.

5 Cfr. George Huber, *Pilgrim of Peace*, Montreal, Palm Publishers, 1967, p. 171.

6 Cfr. Paul VI, *Ecclesiam suam*, in *Acta Apostolicae Sedis,* 56 (1964), no. 70, p. 641. (In the original Latin text of *Ecclesiam suam,* published in *Acta Apostolicae Sedis,* the paragraphs are not numbered. Hence pages are reproduced here after the paragraph numbers. The current paragraph numbers of the encyclical are those found in the official English translation of the Latin text taken from the Vatican

it. The Pope wanted his apostolic ministry to be characterised by dialogue.[7] In fact, his apostolic visits to different countries, and world organisations, were meant to show that his dialogical programme was not purely theoretical.[8]

2. Importance of *Ecclesiam suam* for dialogue

In order to understand Pope Paul VI's views on dialogue, it is necessary to have a thorough knowledge his encyclical *Ecclesiam suam*. It had three aims: a) to promote a *deeper self-knowledge* of the Church;[9] b) to call the Church to a *renewal*;[10] and c) to foster *dialogue* with the world in which she lives and works.[11] The first aim is spiritual, second moral, and third apostolic.[12] The encyclical also served as a form of guidelines for the third (1964) and fourth (1965) sessions of the Vatican II.[13] Thus, since the Vatican II, the Church started

---

Website. Cfr. http://www.vatican.va/holy_father/paul_vi/encyclicals/documents/hf_p-vi_enc_06081964_ecclesiam_en.html (14.2. 2015).

7 Cfr. Paul VI, *Ecclesiam suam*, no. 67, p. 640.

8 Pope Paul VI made nine pastoral journeys: 1) in January 1964 he visited the Holy Land, Israel; 2) in December 1964 he stopped in Lebanon on his way to Bombay (Mumbai), India, for the International Eucharistic Congress; 3) in 1965 he addressed the General Assembly of the United Nations and concluded his visit to New York by celebrating a mass at Yankee Stadium; 4) in 1967 he made a pilgrimage to Fatima, Portugal; 5) in July 1967 he visited Istanbul, Turkey; 6) in August 1968 he participated in the International Eucharistic Congress at Bogota, Columbia; 7) in 1969 he travelled to Switzerland; 8) in July 1969 he visited Uganda; 9) in 1970 he travelled to Fareast, his longest journey, stopping at Teheran, Karachi, Manila, Samoa, Australia, Jakarta and Sri Lanka. Cfr. P. Granfield, "Paul VI, Pope", in *New Catholic Encyclopedia*, Vol. 11, Washington, Gale, 2003[2] p. 31.

9 Cfr. Paul VI, *Ecclesiam suam*, no. 9, p. 611; no. 18, pp. 614-615.

10 Cfr. Ibid., no. 11, p. 612.

11 Cfr. Ibid., no. 12, p. 612.

12 Cfr. *Insegnamenti di Paolo VI*, Vol. II, Città del Vaticano, Tipografia Poliglotta Vaticana, 1964, p. 473.

13 Cfr. Paul VI, *Ecclesiam suam*, no. 66, p. 640. *Ecclesiamn suam* undoubtedly influenced a number of documents that the Second Vatican Council produced, especially *Gaudium et spes, Nostra aetate, Lumen gentium, Ad gentes* and *Unitatis redintegratio*.

speaking about the 'era of dialogue', and considered dialogue as one of the ways of spreading the salvific message of the Gospel, thanks to *Ecclesiam suam*.

The Pope says that, dialogue is a necessity in a pluralistic society, and human beings have attained a level of maturity so that, whether people are religious or not, their secular education has enabled them to think, speak and conduct a dialogue with dignity.[14] Besides, the fact that Christians are distinct from the world does not mean that they are entirely separated from it or indifferent to it or afraid of it, or contemptuous of it, but go closer to it.[15] It encyclical affirms that, the Church is ready to dialogue with all people of good will, both inside and outside the Church, and none will be excluded from it.[16]

Ecclesiam suam does not deal with any particular theological or doctrinal matter, but the *method* which the Church should follow in order to walk according to the will of Christ. In fact, the Pope says that, the encyclical can be given the title 'the ways of the Church' (*le vie della Chiesa*).[17] Dialogue is, therefore, the method, mode, art and style of the Church in her apostolic activities.[18] In a sense, it was also a declaration of the policies of the pontificate of Paul VI.[19] He said: "[...] no other course is open to Us in view of Our conviction that it is this kind of dialogue that will characterize Our apostolic ministry."[20] His other encyclicals, apostolic exhortations and numerous homilies

---

14 Cfr. Ibid., no. 78, p. 644.

15 Cfr. Ibid., no. 63, pp. 638-639.

16 Cfr. Ibid., nos. 93, 94, p. 649.

17 Cfr. *Insegnamenti di Paolo VI*, Vol. II, p. 473.

18 Cfr. Ibid.

19 Cfr. Paul VI, *Ecclesiam suam*, no. 4, p. 610. On 22 June 1973, on the tenth anniversary of his election as Pope, in his address to the college of cardinals he declared that dialogue with all peoples has been the programme of his pontificate, as expressed in his first encyclical *Ecclesiam suam*. Cfr. *Insegnamenti di Paolo VI*, Vol. XI, Città del Vaticano, Tipografia Poliglotta Vaticana, 1973, p. 634.

20 Paul VI, *Ecclesiam suam*, no. 67, p. 640. In *Ecclesiam suam* Pope Paul VI uses majestic plural.

and discourses would enrich and complement the ideas on dialogue contained in *Eccleaism suam.*[21]

3. Meaning of dialogue

Dialogue is an interpersonal communication which has a complex structure and assumes multiple forms. Pope Paul VI describes dialogue as an *interior impulse of charity* which tends towards expressing itself.[22] Dialogue is an attitude of *searching for truth* in the other and in oneself. Therefore, sincere dialogue has only one aim, namely common love of truth.[23] The Pope says: "[...] dialogue is not an end but a means. It does not give the truth, but seeks it. It is a method and not a system."[24] Dialogue is also a *mental attitude* which the Church should adopt regarding the contemporary world.[25]

According to the Pope, the dialogue of a Christian has to be *dialogue of salvation.*[26] It presupposes a state of mind on the part of a Christian who realises the seriousness of the apostolic mission as a baptised person, and sees one's own salvation as inseparable from the salvation of others.[27] Dialogue is therefore a preferred *method* in the apostolate and a way of making spiritual contact with others.[28]

4. Theological foundations of dialogue

Pope Paul VI maintained that, the plan of God for humanity unfolds itself in the form of a great dialogue, and has its foundation in the

21 Pope Paul VI's entire magisterium is available in sixteen volumes entitled *Insegnamenti di Paolo VI* (1963-1978) published by Tipografia Poliglotta Vaticana, Città del Vaticano.

22 Cfr. Paul VI, *Ecclesiam suam*, no. 64, p. 639.

23 Cfr. Jean Guitton, *The Pope Speaks. Dialogues of Paul VI with Jean Guitton*, Anne and Christopher Fremantle (tr.), New York, Meredith Press, 1968, pp. 162, 167.

24 Ibid. p. 166.

25 Cfr. Paul VI, *Ecclesiam suam*, no. 58, p. 637.

26 Cfr. Ibid., no. 73, p. 642.

27 Cfr. Ibid., no. 80, p. 644.

28 Cfr. Ibid., no. 81, p. 644.

mind of God.[29] *Religion* of its very nature is a certain relationship between God and human beings, and it finds its expression in prayer, and prayer is a dialogue.[30] God's *revelation* is dialogue with the human race, and it establishes a supernatural relationship between God and human beings, and likewise looked upon as dialogue.[31] In the *Incarnation* of Jesus Christ and in the *Gospel* it is God's Word that speaks to us.[32] Dialogue has a *Trinitarian foundation* because it is God the Father who initiates the dialogue with the human race, and it is established through Christ in the Holy Spirit.[33] The whole *history of salvation* is one long dialogue, which marvellously begins with God and which He prolongs with human beings in so many different ways.[34] Thus, Paul VI affirms that, dialogue has a transcendental foundation because its source is in God himself.

Paul VI spoke of an *anthropological foundation* for dialogue when he affirmed that, all things human are the concern of Christians, and that Christians share with the whole human race a common nature, and a common life with all its gifts and its problems.[35] Dialogue is founded on the *theology of charity*, because the internal drive of charity always seeks external expressions, and dialogue is one of them.[36]

The theology of dialogue has an *eschatological dimension* because God's dialogue with human beings is a *dialogue of salvation* (*colloquium salutis*), and it is He who takes the initiative in it because it is He who has loved us first.[37] Dialogue originates from the goodness and love of God.[38] But this dialogue does not depend on the merits of those with

29 Cfr. Ibid., no. 70, p. 641.

30 Cfr. Ibid.

31 Cfr. Ibid.

32 Cfr. Ibid.

33 Cfr. Ibid., no. 71, p. 642.

34 Cfr. Ibid., no. 70, p. 641.

35 Cfr. Ibid., no. 97, p. 650.

36 Cfr. Ibid., no. 64, p. 639.

37 Cfr. Ibid., no. 72, p. 642.

38 Cfr. Ibid., no. 73, p. 642.

whom it is initiated, nor on the results it is likely to achieve. Dialogue of salvation thrives in a climate of friendship and service.[39] Since 'God so loved the world as to give his only begotten Son' (Jn 3:16), nothing but unselfish love should motivate Christian dialogue.[40] The Church offers the gift of salvation to all through dialogue, without making any distinction, and respecting the personal and civic rights of the individuals. It does not use physical force or external coercion, but appeals to human friendliness and interior persuasion, and leaves people free to respond to it or reject it.[41] Dialogue of salvation develops gradually and progressively. It has humble beginning in small things. It takes cognizance of the slowness of human psychological and historical maturation, and waits for the hour when God may make the dialogue effective.[42] Every form of dialogue of the Church has to be a dialogue of salvation because it is a continuation of the dialogue of God with humanity. Conversion of others to the Christian faith is not the immediate object of dialogue.[43]

5. The four concentric circles of dialogue

Pope Paul VI envisaged four concentric circles of dialogue. The first comprises the *entire human race* or the world as a whole, and therefore, this circle is immense.[44] Here, dialogue is carried out with all people of good will, who with a sincere heart are in search of the truth and study ways to improve the well-being of humanity. Some of them often serve a noble cause for the progress of society and betterment of human beings, which they consider as the ultimate of perfection.[45] Sometimes one finds among them people of great breadth of mind, who are impatient with mediocrity and self-

39 Cfr. Ibid., no. 87, p. 647.

40 Cfr. Ibid., no. 73, p. 642.

41 Cfr. Ibid., no. 75, pp. 642-743.

42 Cfr. Ibid., no. 77, p. 643.

43 Cfr. Ibid., no. 79, p. 644.

44 Cfr. Ibid., no. 97, p. 650.

45 Cfr. Ibid., no. 104, pp. 652-653.

seeking.[46] In this circle one may also find people who profess no religion at all, and subscribe to atheism in one of its many different forms,[47] and communist ideologies which deny God and oppress the Church.[48] The Pope says that, dialogue with them is difficult, but not impossible.[49] Then there are situations in which there is absence of sufficient freedom of thought and action, and in such cases dialogue is not possible, and one can only practice silence, and even if one attempts at dialogue, it will only be a voice crying in the wilderness. But the Pope says that, the silence is already a witness of the faith of the Church.[50] He also adds that, the Church does not give up the hope of the eventual possibility of a dialogue between the atheists, and the atheistic political and philosophical systems.[51]

The second circle consists of all those *people who worship the one supreme God.*[52] This is also a very vast field, and consists of all those who believe in a God who is acknowledged as a transcendent being. First, the Jewish people who retain the religion of the Old Testament, then those worshippers who adhere to other monotheistic religions, especially the Muslims, and then the followers of the great Afro-Asiatic religions.[53] This is the area of *interreligious dialogue.* But the Pope affirms that, as Christians, we cannot agree with these various forms of religion, nor can we adopt an indifferent or uncritical attitude towards them on the assumption that, all religions are equal.[54] At the same time, Christians cannot turn a blind eye to the spiritual and moral values found in these non-Christian religions.[55]

---

46 Cfr. Ibid., no. 104, p. 653.

47 Cfr. Ibid., no. 99, pp. 650-651.

48 Cfr. Ibid., no. 101, pp. 651-652.

49 Cfr. Ibid., no. 102, p. 652.

50 Cfr. Ibid., nos. 102-103, p. 652.

51 Cfr. Ibid., nos. 104-105, pp. 653-654.

52 Cfr. Ibid., no. 107, p. 654.

53 Cfr. Ibid., no. 107, pp. 654-655.

54 Cfr. Ibid., no. 107, p. 655.

55 Cfr. Ibid., no. 108, p. 655.

The third circle embraces *Christians,* that is, those who have heard the call of Christ and who recognize him as God.[56] But within the circle of Christians there are further circles, like the Orthodox Christians and the Christians of the reformed Christian communities.[57] Here, believers in Christ should stress what they all have in common rather than what divides them. This is the field of *ecumenical dialogue.*[58] Paul VI declared that, he is ready to examine how the Catholic Church can meet the legitimate desires of the separated Christians on the points of difference concerning tradition, spirituality, canon law and worship.[59]

The fourth circle covers those who belong to the *one, holy, catholic and apostolic Church of which the Roman Church* is mother and head. Here, according to Paul VI, the purpose of dialogue is that they may come to the fullness of faith, charity and holiness, and be open and responsive to all truth, every virtue and every spiritual value.[60] This is the sector of *dialogue within the Church.* The Pope says that, the dialogue between the members of a Christian community should be founded on love. The right to command and the duty to obey must be present in any properly constituted society, especially in the Church. The exercise of authority needs to be carried out in a spirit of dialogue, service, truth and charity, and obedience to lawful authority should be based on faith, freedom, respect and serenity. But a spirit of independence, bitter criticism, defiance and arrogance completely vitiates dialogue and turns it into argument, disagreement and dissension.[61] The Church should become a place where there is

---

56 Cfr Ibid., no. 109, p. 655.

57 Cfr Jean Guitton, *The Pope Speaks. Dialogues of Paul VI with Jean Guitton*, pp. 171-172.

58 Cfr. Paul VI, *Ecclesiam suam*, no. 109, p. 655.

59 Cfr. Ibid., no. 109, p. 655. It is important to note that, in *Ecclesiam suam* Pope Paul VI reaffirmed Petrine primacy, and declared that it will not be sacrificed for the sake of reconciliation among the separated Christians. Cfr. Ibid, no. 110, p. 656.

60 Cfr. Ibid., no. 113, p. 657.

61 Cfr. Ibid., nos. 114-115, pp. 657-658.

health-giving dialogue between priests, religious and laity under the guidance of competent ecclesiastical authority.[62]

6. Creation of permanent structures for dialogue

Paul VI created a number of permanent structures to carry out dialogue at different levels and with different categories of people. On 17 May 1964, Pentecost Sunday, he announced his intention to establish a Secretariat for Non-Christians.[63] Two days later on 19 May, it was officially instituted, and on that occasion he said: "While Vatican Council II is in progress, We thought it useful to institute a special council or secretariat with the task of turning its wholesome attention to those who are without Christian religion, and to whom it would however seem that the words of the Lord refer 'I have other sheep that do not belong to this fold. These also I must lead' (Jn 10:16)." [64] The aim of the Secretariat is to promote mutual knowledge, collaboration and dialogue between the members of different religious traditions of the world, and to enhance and defend the ideals of religious freedom, brotherhood, good culture, social welfare, and civil order.[65] Other structures he created for dialogue are the following: on 7 April 1965 the Secretariat for Non-Believers; on 6 January 1967 the Pontifical Commission for Laity, and the Pontifical Commission for Justice and Peace. He also endorsed the already existing Secretariat for Promoting Christian Unity established by his predecessor Pope John XXIII on 5 June 1960.[66] On 22 October 1974 he established two commissions to promote dialogue with Jews and

62 Cfr. Ibid., no. 116, p. 659.

63 Cfr. *Insegnamenti di Paolo VI,* Vol. II, p. 342.

64 Paul VI, *Progrediente Concilio,* in *Acta Apostolicae Sedis,* 56 (1964), p. 560. This English translation is from Pontifical Council for Interreligious Dialogue, *The Official Teachings of the Catholic Church from the Second Vatican Council to John Paul II (1963-2005*), Francesco Gioia (ed.), Boston, Pauline Books and Media, 2006, pp. 69-70.

65 Cfr. *Insegnamenti di Paolo VI,* Vol. XII, p. 638.

66 http://www.vatican.va/roman_curia/pontifical_councils/chrstuni/documents/rc_pc_chrstuni_pro_20051996_chrstuni_pro_en.html (9.10.2014).

Muslims: the Commission for Religious Relations with Jews, and the Commission for Religious Relations with Muslims. They came under, respectively, the Secretariat for Promoting Christian Unity, and the Secretariat for Non-Christians.[67]

7. Conditions for dialogue

Pope Paul VI proposed certain conditions for a fruitful dialogue. The principal ones are the following: *First*, since Christians believe that, God took the initiative to dialogue with the human race, they must be the first to take the initiative for dialogue with others, and should not wait to be summoned to it by others.[68] *Second*, a Christian should enter into dialogue impelled by sincere and ardent love and not by any other motive.[69] *Third*, there should be an atmosphere of charity and truth because without love there cannot be knowledge of the other, and truth is intrinsically wedded to charity,[70] and charity manifests itself in courteous esteem, understanding and goodness on the part of the one who initiates the dialogue. It avoids *a priori* condemnation, bigotry, prejudice, malicious and indiscriminate hostility, polemic and empty, boastful speech.[71] *Fourth*, some basic convergences or something common must exist between partners before dialogue can begin. The Pope says that, the foundation for a fruitful dialogue is stressing what people have in common with each other rather than what divides them.[72] *Fifth*, there should be no compulsion so that no one feels forced into dialogue, but invited under the influence of love.[73] Sixth, dialogue does not presuppose

67 Cfr. Michael L. Fitzgerald and John Borelli, *Interfaith Dialogue. A Catholic View*, New York, Orbis Books, 2006, p. 241.

68 Cfr. Paul VI, *Ecclesiam suam*, no. 72, p. 642.

69 Cfr. Ibid., no. 73, p. 642.

70 Cfr. Ibid., no. 82, p. 645.

71 Cfr. Ibid., no. 79, p. 644.

72 Cfr. Ibid., no. 109, p. 655.

73 Cfr Ibid., no. 75, p. 642.

equality between the partners.[74] *Seventh*, dialogue should be adapted to the intelligence of those to whom it is addressed, and must take into account the different circumstances and cultural backgrounds of people. For example, the Pope says that, dialogue with children is not the same as dialogue with adults, nor is dialogue with Christians same as dialogue with non-believers.[75] *Eighth*, dialogue requires humility and simplicity: in order to dialogue effectively one needs to identify oneself with others, imitating Christ who became man and identified himself with humanity. One must forego all privileges and adapt oneself to the way of life of the most humble people, if one wishes to be listened to and understood. Before speaking one must take great care to listen not only to what people say, but more especially to what they have in their hearts to say. Only then can one understand them and respect them, and even as far as possible, agree with them.[76]

8. Aims of dialogue

According to Paul VI, every authentic dialogue is inspired by sincere *love for truth*, and truth is attainable by searching and learning together. It is in the process of dialogue that a Christian will discover elements of truth in others, and express the Christian teachings and doctrines in such a way that others can respond to them. The result of this is *deeper knowledge* of each other and *wider exposure*.[77] Dialogue can promote *justice and peace and eradication of evil, misfortunes and miseries* afflicting millions of people all over the world. The Pope says: "Our mission is to bring men [people] together in mutual love through the power of that kingdom of justice, and peace which

---

74 When Jean Guitton objected to it, the Pope said: "According to you [Guitton] then, no dialogue is possible between son and father, disciple and master; and, especially, between a layman and the Pope." Jean Guitton, *The Pope Speaks. Dialogues of Paul VI with Jean Guitton*, p. 167.

75 Cfr. Paul VI, *Ecclesiam suam*, no. 78, p. 644.

76 Cfr. Ibid., no. 87, pp. 646-647.

77 Cfr. Ibid., no. 83, p. 646.

Christ inaugurated by His coming into the world."[78] Dialogue aims at *cultivation of charity* expressed towards God and the whole human race, and such charity manifests itself in religious and moral values, and in the practical situations of daily life.[79] Through dialogue it is possible to promote and defend common ideals such as religious freedom, human brotherhood, education, culture, social welfare and civic order.[80] Paul VI was convinced that, dialogue is possible in all these great projects, which is the concern of both Christians and non-Christians.[81]

9. Dialogue as a method of accomplishing Church's mission

According to Paul VI, the task of the Church is to serve society[82] because the Church is deeply rooted in the world, it exists in the world, draws its members from it, it derives from it a wealth of human culture, and shares its vicissitudes and promotes its prosperity.[83] Hence the Church cannot remain indifferent to or unaffected by the changes which take place in the world. The Church must not only adapt itself to the forms of thought and living, provided such forms are not incompatible with the basic principles of its religious and moral teaching, but must also strive to approach these forms and to correct, ennoble, encourage and sanctify them.[84] Therefore, it is necessary that the Church enters into dialogue with the world in which it lives because it has something to say, a message to give, and a communication to make.[85] It will approach secular society with a view to exercising a positive influence over it.[86] Thus, dialogue

78 Ibid., no. 16, p. 614.

79 Cfr. Ibid., no. 56, pp. 635-636.

80 Cfr. Ibid., no. 108, p. 655.

81 Cfr. Ibid.

82 Cfr. Ibid., no. 5, p. 610.

83 Cfr. Ibid., no. 26, p. 617.

84 Cfr. Ibid., no. 42, pp. 627-628.

85 Cfr. Ibid., no. 65, p. 639.

86 Cfr. Ibid., no. 78, p. 643.

becomes one of the important methods of accomplishing the mission of the Church in the world.

10. Characteristics of dialogue

Dialogue, which is a recognised method of the Church's apostolic mission, should have certain characteristics: In *Ecclesiam suam* Paul VI discusses four main characteristics of genuine dialogue, namely, clarity, meekness, confidence and prudence. We shall discuss them briefly:

10.1 Clarity

According to Paul VI, since genuine dialogue is an exercise of the highest spiritual and mental powers of a person, and one of the greatest manifestations of human activity and culture, it should be intelligible and easily understandable, and calls for an examination of the kind of speech one uses.[87] It should be adapted to the partner's mentality, to his or her notions and way of thinking, and should use terms which everyone can understand. He considered affirming one's deepest convictions and fundamental beliefs in absolute sincerity, the courage to express what is in one's mind as well as in the heart, investigating to find out better ways of expressing oneself, great fairness in expounding one's doctrines, and taking utmost care to listen not only what others have to say and but also what they have in their hearts to say, also as belonging to the sphere clarity. [88]

10.2 Meekness

Dialogue needs to be accompanied by meekness. This quality refers to the way of speaking as well as behaviour. Meekness demands avoidance of any authoritarian or domineering attitude in the way of expressing one's ideas. It does not impose anything on others, and rejects any form of fanaticism, violence, bitterness, arrogance and hardness of speech. It admits criticism and manifests one's large-

87 Cfr. Ibid., no. 81, pp. 644-645.

88 Cfr. Ibid., nos. 83, 87, pp. 646-647.

mindedness and makes no demands on others. It is patient under contradiction, charitable and generous;[89] it is peaceful, excludes all pretence, rivalry, deceit and betrayal, and fosters a disinterested, objective and sincere dialogue.[90]

10.3 Confidence

Dialogue is to be marked by confidence in the rightness of one's truths and values. It implies confidence in the good will of the parties engaged in dialogue. A dialogue carried out in confidence promotes intimacy and friendship, and trust on both sides. It unites them in a mutual adherence to the Good, and excludes all self-seeking.[91] Confidence also means certainty in reaching the aims of dialogue.

10.4 Prudence

Prudence as a characteristic of dialogue esteems highly the psychological and moral circumstances of the partner in dialogue, whether he or she is a child, uneducated, unprepared, diffident or hostile. A prudent person strives to make allowances to the sensitivities of the listener, and adapts oneself and the manner of one's presentation in a reasonable way, lest one be displeasing and incomprehensible to the listener.[92]

10.5 Other characteristics

Dialogue demands attachment and *fidelity to one's own faith*, and under no circumstance it can dispense a Christian from the obligation of observing his or her faith.[93] Dialogue has to be carried out with *dignity* as people today are more conscious of their worth and uniqueness than before.[94] It needs to be as *universal* as possible

89 Cfr. Ibid., no. 81, p. 645.

90 Cfr. Ibid., no. 106, p. 654.

91 Cfr. Ibid., no. 81, p. 645.

92 Cfr. Ibid., no. 81, p. 645; no. 106, p. 654; no. 109, p. 656.

93 Cfr. Ibid., no. 88, p. 647.

94 Cfr. Ibid., nos. 78-79, p. 644.

without excluding anyone, not even the opponents of the Church or her persecutors.[95] Dialogue is carried out with an attitude of *disinterestedness* and devoid of any temporal or political motive.[96] Dialogue is *meant for all*, and the Pope encouraged all the baptised to take part in it. In a special way he invited priests, religious and lay persons engaged in Catholic Action, other associations, and different apostolic activities of the Church, to dedicate themselves to it. But he also added that, it must be done *under the guidance of competent authority* in the Church.[97]

11. Dangers in dialogue

Paul VI says that, the desire to come together as brothers and sisters for dialogue must not lead to a watering down or subtracting from the truth. It should not weaken one's attachment to one's faith and must not lead to vague compromises concerning the principles of Christian faith, both in theory and practice. One needs to avoid the temptation to make peace and sink differences at all costs. The Pope adds that, only a person who is totally faithful to the teaching of Christ can be an apostle, and only one who lives one's Christian life to the full can remain uncontaminated by the errors with which one comes into contact. Hence, dialogue requires great wisdom, prudence, patience and openness to the voice of the Spirit so as not to fall into syncretism and irenicism.[98] In dialogue one must also guard against the danger of relativism.[99]

---

95 Cfr. Ibid., no. 76, p. 643.

96 Cfr. Ibid., no. 98, p. 650.

97 Cfr. Ibid., no. 116, p. 659.

98 Cfr. Ibid., no. 88, p. 647. The term 'irenicism' is derived from the Greek *eirene* meaning 'peace'. Irenicism in Christian theology refers to attempts to unify Christian apologetical systems by using reason as an essential attribute. Cfr. http://en.wikipedia.org/wiki/Irenicism (14.10.2014)

99 Cfr. Paul VI, *Ecclesiam suam*, no. 87, p. 646.

12. Fruits of dialogue

Dialogue can lead to greater mutual understanding, enrichment, co-operation, removal of prejudices and misunderstanding, discovery of differences and new truth. It can promote and defend universal values like, justice, peace, unity, brotherhood, liberty, interreligious harmony, mutual love and respect among people of different cultures, civic and moral order, communion of life and creation of a better world.[100] Peace is one of the precious fruits of dialogue. Dialogue has the capacity to favour free and honourable peace free from all pretence, rivalry, deceit and betrayal. It can bring people together at every level: heads of States, the body of a nation and its foundations, whether social, family or individual, and can inspire in every institution and every person the understanding and love of peace and the duty to defend it.[101]

13. Missionary apostolate retains its supreme value

Though in *Ecclesiam suam* great emphasis is laid on dialogue, the supreme value of missionary evangelisation is retained with greatest clarity. The encyclical unequivocally affirms that, proclamation of the Word is the primary mission of the Church.[102] This is because, the Church has a clear awareness of a mission received from God and of a message to be spread far and wide. There is an evangelical duty and a mandate to teach all nations in order to offer eternal salvation to all peoples. The final command of Christ to His apostles was 'go therefore and make disciples of all nations' (Mt 28,19), and it implies a mission from which there is no escaping.[103] Paul VI says: "We want to stress once more the very important place that preaching still has, especially in the modern Catholic apostolate and in connection with the dialogue which is Our present concern. No

---

100 Cfr. Ibid., no. 106, p. 654; no. 108, p. 655.

101 Cfr. Ibid., no. 106, p. 654.

102 Cfr. Ibid., no. 90, p. 648.

103 Cfr. Ibid., no. 66, p. 639.

other form of communication can take its place";[104] "Preaching is our primary apostolate. Our ministry, Venerable Brethren, is before all else the ministry of the Word."[105]

14. A critical appreciation

Pope Paul VI is primarily responsible for the radical changes in the approaches and attitudes of the Catholic Church towards world at large, and non-Christian religions in particular. The encyclical *Ecclesiam suam* is considered as the 'roadmap' of his papacy where dialogue figures prominently. The kind of dialogue he advocates is complex, consisting of doctrinal, pastoral, spiritual, human and sociological elements. It is not tactical or dialectical, but simple and practical, respectful and open. The encyclical also anticipated some of the great themes that were to appear in the documents of the Vatican II, and urged the Church to have a greater *awareness* of herself, to undertake the necessary *reform* and establish a *dialogue* with the world. In this sense it was a very significant and ground-breaking document.

14.1 As a method dialogue was not anything new

The method of dialogue which Paul VI proposed for the Catholic Church was not anything new in the history of the Church. It was already present in different forms and degrees in the Old and the New Testaments, in the life of Jesus, Apostles, Fathers of the Church, missionaries, and simple Christians, and has been enhanced throughout the centuries. But in the Second Vatican Council, dialogue was *explicitly proposed and officially confirmed as a pastoral method* of the Church, and Paul VI played a decisive role in it. His encyclical *Ecclesiam suam* appeared before the Conciliar documents that formally discuss dialogue, and it greatly influenced the conciliar debates on the issue.[106] The originality of Paul VI consists in this.

104 Ibid., no. 90, p. 648.

105 Ibid.

106 Cfr. Krystian Gawron, *Dialogue in the Teachings of Pope Paul VI*, London, Veritas, 1993, pp. 225-226.

14.2 Paul VI's idea of dialogue was earlier than that of Vatican II

From where did Paul VI take the idea of dialogue? What factors influenced him? Why did he decide to propose the idea to the whole Church? Though these questions are not easy to answer, one could identify such factors as, the environment and family climate of his childhood, priestly formation, work in the Vatican Secretariat of State, journeys to different countries before becoming Pope, teachings of his immediate predecessor Popes, especially Leo XIII, Pius XI, Benedict XV, Pius XII and John XXIII, vast reading and personal study, his open nature and contact with others, etc. And yet, as Krystian Gawron maintains, Paul VI remained in a very evident way, the author of his ideas, teaching and activity.[107] *Ecclesiam suam* published in 1964 opened up the whole Church to the enriching dialogical co-operation, not only within the local Churches, but also with the entire world, and this was *before* the Vatican II documents that discuss dialogue appeared. Hence, the Pope's concept of dialogue was earlier than that of the Second Vatican Council.[108]

14.3 Paul VI's idea of dialogue is wider than that of Vatican II

Paul VI's had a much richer and wider idea of dialogue than that which is found in the early documents of the Vatican II, which for the most part, is limited to doctrinal dialogue of speculative nature. But in those documents that were debated and approved *after* the publication of *Ecclesiam suam*, one notices a more comprehensive meaning of the term. The best developed idea of dialogue may be found in the later chronological conciliar documents, like *Nostra aetate, Unitatis redintegratio* and *Gaudium et spes.* At the same time, it is also to be stated that, although the council accepted the concept of 'dialogue', it did it with some reserve, so that the term refers basically to dialogue as a method of searching for the truth, a way of co-operation for the common good, and a style of living in communion

107 Cfr. Ibid., p. 227.

108 Cfr. Ibid., p. 229.

with people. In this sense, the council took only a partial idea of dialogue from the Pope.[109]

14.4 Dialogue is an integral part of evangelisation

For Paul VI, dialogue of the Church is essentially a dialogue of salvation, which is to be carried out at world level, excluding no one. For him the method of dialogue is a way of carrying out the work of evangelisation, because according to his theology of dialogue, every act of dialogue is a dialogue of salvation. But dialogue is not a substitute for missionary evangelisation. Though the Church promotes dialogue, it still retains the primacy of missionary apostolate.[110]

14.5 Conversion is not ruled out in dialogue

Paul VI maintains that, though conversion of others to the Christian faith is not the immediate object of dialogue,[111] it is not ruled out. According to him, Christianity is the only true faith[112], and when the Christian's partner in dialogue freely decides to accept for himself or herself all the essential Christian values, because he or she finds them the most desirable and suitable, dialogue assumes its deepest pastoral meaning, and here one deals with real conversion. A Christian engaged in dialogue with a person of another faith should help him or her in this process with a fuller sharing of ideas and convictions.[113] Here, as a criticism, it needs to be stated that, this can lead to reluctance on the part of non-Christians to participate in dialogue, or interpret dialogue as a new method invented by the Church to get converts to the Christian faith.

---

109 Cfr. Ibid.

110 Cfr. Paul VI, *Ecclesiam suam*, no. 90, p. 648.

111 Cfr. Ibid., no. 79, p. 644.

112 Cfr. Ibid.

113 Cfr. Ibid.

14.6 Need for a critical attitude towards non-Christian religions

Although the Pope manifests openness towards non-Christian religions, he is also somewhat critical about them. He affirms that, one cannot agree with all the different forms of religion, nor can adopt an indifferent or uncritical attitude towards them on the assumption that they are all to be treated as equal.[114] What is implied here is that, there are elements in non-Christian religions which may need purification, and that Christianity is superior to other religions. This attitude can also make non-Christians less enthusiastic about engaging in dialogue with Christians.

14.7 Christianity is the true and the most sublime religion

Paul VI argues that, though religions are many and all of them deal with relationship with God, true religion is only one and it is Christianity. According to him, the Christian religion is the true and the most sublime religion, not invented by any human being but revealed by God. He says: "Indeed, honesty compels us to declare openly our conviction that the Christian religion is the one and only true religion."[115] Here it needs to be stated that, non-Christians might interpret this 'exclusiveness' of Christianity as the 'one true religion' as an expression of Christian arrogance.

14.8 A developed theology of dialogue

Ecclesiam suam has a quite well developed theology of dialogue. Paul VI took pains to establish dialogue on solid Trinitarian, Christological, pneumatological, anthropological, ecclesiological and eschatological foundations, and on theology of charity. This is another major achievement of the document. In this sense the encyclical is not only pastoral but also deeply theological, and fully

114 Cfr. Ibid., no. 107, p. 655.

115 Ibid. The Latin text reads: "*Quin immo, sinceritatis officio ducati, ea quae nos credimus, oportet manifestemus, videlicet veram religionem esse unam eamque esse christianam.*"

justifies dialogue as a method envisaged by the Pope for fulfilling the mission of the Church in the modern world.

14.9 Amble freedom for the Council Fathers

The encyclical *Eccesiam suam* was promulgated when the Second Vatican Council was in progress. But Paul VI, as head of the Catholic Church, did not impose his views on dialogue on the Council Fathers, but gave them ample freedom to discuss in detail the ideas contained in his encyclical. He said: "Our only concern, Venerable Brothers, is to propose certain points for your consideration before the beginning of the third session, so that we may all gain a clearer understanding of the compelling motives for Church's dialogue, the methods to be followed and the end in view."[116]

14.10 Some drawbacks of the encyclical

One of the drawbacks of *Ecclesiam suam* is that, it does not have a well-developed theology of religions which is very fundamental for developing a theology of interreligious dialogue. Though Paul VI admits that, religion of its very nature, is a relationship between God and human beings[117] and spiritual and moral values are found in non-Christian religions[118] these ideas are not adequately developed in his encyclical.[119] Dialogue is inspired by sincere love for the truth, and those who engage in dialogue are convinced of it. But in the encyclical this is aspect does not seem have received the attention it deserves. Though the word 'culture' occurs a number of times in the encyclical in different contexts, the intrinsic relationship between religion and culture is not discussed. In the encyclical the

116 Ibid., no. 66, pp. 639-640.

117 Cfr. Ibid., no. 70, p. 641.

118 Cfr. Ibid., no. 108, p. 655.

119 Here one should keep in mind that, *Ecclesiam suam* was the first encyclical of Pope Paul VI, and it is unrealistic to expect a highly developed theology of religions in it, as it was not the scope of the document. But he did develop a rich and well-articulated theology of religions over the years, as is evident from his later encyclicals, apostolic exhortations and discourses.

pneumatological aspect of the theology of dialogue is weak and the anthropological dimension of dialogue is underdeveloped, though he says that 'all things human are our concern'.[120] Finally, on the whole, Paul VI was cautious and rather negative in his approach towards non-Christian religions, with many things in them to be criticised, corrected and purified. He also clearly maintained, and openly stated that, Christianity is superior to all other religions. Such an outspoken statement can have negative impact on interreligious relations, even if as a convinced Christian and head of the Catholic Church, he cannot be expected to hold a position different from this.[121]

15. Conclusion

Pope Paul VI was, in many ways, a 'prophet of dialogue'. With his encyclical *Ecclesiam suam* he initiated a new style of apostolic ministry in the Catholic Church, and manifested his pastoral progressivism and creativity to respond to the signs of the times. He envisaged dialogue as a way of fulfilling his apostolic ministry, and an essential element in the pastoral method of the Church, and therefore, he encouraged it, created institutions for promoting it, and gave personal example in it.[122] Consequently, the attitude of the non-Christian world towards the Church began to change from suspicion to trust. His stressed three key principles in dialogue: dialogue needs deepening of one's Christian identity; dialogue involves the life of the whole Church, and therefore of every Christian; and dialogue should not be divorced from the proclamation of the Gospel. On 25 September 1985 Cardinal Agostino Casaroli (1914-1998), a close friend of Paul VI and former Vatican Secretary of State, while

120 Cfr. Paul VI, *Ecclesiam suam*, no. 97, p. 650.

121 It must be stated that, the conviction of Pope Paul VI about his Christian faith is fully justifiable. In fact, paradoxically, all partners in interreligious dialogue who are convinced of their faith, enter into dialogue with other religions with their 'absolutist views'. But it is also true that, if one over emphasizes one's 'absolutist view', it can be an obstacle to genuine dialogue.

122 Cfr. Marcello Zago, *Buddhismo e Cristianesimo in Dialogo. Situazione, Rapporti, Convergenze*, Roma, Citta Nuova Editrice, 1985, p. 250.

unveiling the statue of Pope Paul VI in the cathedral of Brescia, defined him as 'dialogue'[123] According to Jean Guitton, in his mouth the word 'dialogue' was one of the key terms, and it could be said to sum up his way of thinking, his life of relations with people and his conversation,[124] and he will be remembered as a pontiff who tried to dialogue with all people.[125]

---

123 Cfr. Agostino Cardinale Casaroli, "Paolo VI e il dialogo", *Il Regno*, 19/84, 11 November 1984, p. 594, as cited in Peter Hebblethwaite, *Paul VI The First Modern Pope*, New York, Paulist Press, 1993, p. 6.

124 Cfr. Jean Guitton, *The Pope Speaks. Dialogues of Paul VI with Jean Guitton*, p. 84.

125 Cfr. Ibid., p. 162.

Chapter 3

The Relation of the Church to Non-Christian Religions in *Nostra Aetate* and Other Documents of the Vatican II

The Second Vatican Council (1962-1965) of the Catholic Church is considered by many as the most important religious event of the twentieth century. It was formally inaugurated on 11 October 1962 by Pope John XXIII (1881-1963), and was concluded on 8 December 1965 by Pope Paul VI (1897-1978). There were altogether four sessions, one each year. The council produced sixteen documents[1] covering an extraordinarily wide range of subjects and of various lengths, which differ not only in rank, but also in impact and importance. Several conciliar documents made explicit references to non-Christian religions, and one in particular, *Nostra aetate*

1 The highest in rank are the Constitutions (*Constitutiones*) of which there are only four; next in rank are nine Decrees (*Decreta*), and finally three Declarations (*Declarationes*).

(*NA*, 'In Our times'; Declaration on the Relation of the Church to non-Christian Religions, 28 October 1965). This chapter examines the relation of the Church to non-Christian religions according to Vatican II, with special reference to *Nostra aetate,* and its pastoral and theological implications for interreligious dialogue with some critical reflections.

1. Non-Christian religions in *Nostra aetate*

One of the epoch-making breakthroughs during the Second Vatican Council was establishing a positive relationship with non-Christian religions. Until then, the Catholic Church was not officially interested in a dialogical relationship with other religions, and, consequently, had not produced any positive official document on this topic. But with *Nostra aetate* the Church initiated an important beginning, and spoke officially about other religions as entities which the Church should respect and appreciate, and with which Christians should enter into dialogue and collaboration.

1.1 A historical background to *Nostra aetate*

The role that the great religions of the world play in God's saving plan is one of the most challenging questions facing Christianity today. It is surprising to know that, in the original plan of Vatican II, a declaration on non-Christian religions was not contemplated.[2] None planned anything like *Nostra aetate*. Instead Pope John XXIII simply wanted a statement on the Jews, one that would address the evils of anti-Semitism, and appended to the Decree on Ecumenism. The specific and immediate stimulus for this was an audience that he had granted to the Jewish scholar and French historian Jules Isaac (1877-1963). Cardinal Augustin Bea (1881-1968), who was the

2 The Preparatory Commissions of the Vatican II were to deal only with the following topics: 1) Doctrine (Holy Office); 2) Bishops; 3) Oriental Churches; 4) Sacraments; 5) Discipline of Clergy and Laity; 6) Religious Orders: 7) Missions; 8) Liturgy; 9) Seminaries and Catholic Schools; and 10) Lay Apostolate. Cfr. John W. O'Malley, *What Happened at Vatican II*, Massachusetts, The Belknap Press of Harvard University Press, 2008, p. 101.

head of the newly created Vatican Secretariat for Christian Unity, also met with Nahum Goldman (1895-1982), president of the World Jewish Congress and co-chair of the World Conference of Jewish Organisation. Other factors were also at work: earlier in 1960, Ernst Vogt (1903-1984), a Swiss Jesuit and Rector of the *Biblicum*, Rome, had sent a petition to the central preparatory commission of the council, signed by himself and eighteen members of the faculty, asking that the council address the problem of anti-Semitism. Prior to the council, Jacques Maritain (1882-1973) and a few other Roman Catholics, mostly converts from Judaism, had been working for greater understanding between the two faiths, and among them Johannes Marin Oesterreicher (1904-1993), an Austrian Jew who converted to Roman Catholicism and became an ordained priest, was particularly important. During the council, he was a member of Cardinal Bea's Secretariat for Christian unity.[3] Because of the pressure from the Arab world, the document treated not just Jews, but also Muslims. The expressed desire of many Asian bishops led to the explicit mention of Hinduism and Buddhism. In the end, the expanded document with a radically broadened perspective took into consideration all the non-Christian religions. Thus, the effort to produce a statement on Judaism led, *almost by chance*, to a short text on 'all religions'. This 'providential afterthought' turned out to be one of the greatest achievements of Vatican II.[4]

It is also to be remembered that, *Nostra aetate* was the result of over four 'tumultuous' years of struggle. Its 'troubled' history[5], and the opposition faced by the text from several quarters, had a

---

3 Cfr. Ibid., pp. 219-220; Richard R. Gaillardetz and Catherine E. Clifford, *Keys to the Council. Unlocking the Teachings of Vatican II*, Minnesota, Liturgical Press, 2012, pp. 180-183; Karl Rahner und Herbert Vorgrimler, *Kleines Konzilskompendium*, Freiburg, Herder, 1966, pp. 349-350.

4 Cfr. Edward P. Hahnenberg, *A Concise Guide to the Documents of Vatican II*, Cincinnati, Franciscan Media, 2007, p. 156.

5 For a concise history of *Nostra aetate* see Bruno Hussar, "Genesi storica alla dichiarazione conciliare 'Nostra aetate'", in *La Dichiarazione su "Le Relazioni della Chiesa con le Religioni non Cristiane". Genesi e Storia*, Torino, Elle Di Ci, 1986, pp. 22-46.

positive result. In fact, right from the start, the document faced opposition from various quarters for reasons which ranged from pastoral, political, theological to sheer disinterest in non-Christian religions. Some began to ask: why was the council dealing with the issue of non-Christians at all? It had been absent from the agenda of the council before it opened. For many of the bishops from Europe and North America, relations with the Jewish people were of particular interest, especially as a consequence of their treatment by the Germans during the Second World War. But Bishops from other parts of the world found it difficult to understand what the fuss was all about since many of them had very few Jews in their countries and only a vague knowledge of the horrors of the holocaust. The Eastern rite patriarchs from Middle East did not want any positive statement on the Jews for they feared that the Arab nations would see in it a political move favouring the State of Israel, and feared that the Christian minorities in these countries might have to suffer as a consequence. The Arab world made diplomatic pressures on Vatican to prevent any positive statement being made about the Jews. They viewed any support for the Jewish community as a political matter in support of the State of Israel, and not as a religious one. In the early months of 1965 street demonstrations against the document broke out in some cities of the Middle East. A small conservative minority of bishops from Italy, Spain and Latin America expressed the view that an anti-Jewish position was an integral part of Catholic tradition supported by the Scriptures, and could not be reversed. Bishops from Asia and Africa demanded that the Church must speak not only of its relationship with Jewish people but also about the other religions to which two-thirds of the world's population belong.[6] This situation forced Vatican II to consider entirely new horizons.

There were a number of factors that helped to overcome the opposition and create a positive attitude towards the draft on *Nostra*

6 Cfr. John W. O'Malley, *What Happened at Vatican II*, pp. 220-223, 250; Edward Idris Cassidy, *Ecumenism and Interreligious Dialogue, Unitatis Redintegratio, Nostra Aetate*, New York, Paulist Press, 2005, pp. 1267-128; Richard R. Gaillardetz and Catherine E. Clifford, *Keys to the Council*, pp. 180-183.

aetate. In April 1963 Pope John XXIII published the encyclical *Pacem in terris* (11 April 1963) in which he spoke of the human right to worship God 'according to the dictates of an upright conscience' (no. 14). The creation of the Secretariat for Non-Christians by Pope Paul VI in 1964, the publication of the encyclical *Ecclesiam suam* on dialogue (including dialogue with non-Christians) in the same year, the pope's visit to the Holy Land and India, again in the same year, and his meeting with leaders of non-Christian religions there, etc., served the council with a positive incentive to look beyond the narrow confines of the Western world and to think of the Church's relations in terms not only of the Jewish question but also of religions the world over.[7] Thus, as Cardinal Augustin Bea pointed out during one of the sessions of the council, 'what began as a small mustard seed had grown to become a tree in which all religions could build their nests.'[8]

1.2 Contents of *Nostra aetate*

Nostra aetate is by far the shortest document issued by the Second Vatican Council. It opens with 'In our times' (*Nostra aetate*), words by which the text is known today, and is divided into five sections (five numbered paragraph groups). The first three sections are a brief but positive appraisal of Hinduism, Buddhism and other religions in general, and a relatively long appraisal on Muslims. The fourth section is dedicated to Catholic-Jewish relations, followed by the fifth section, which forms the conclusion.

7 Cfr. Jacques Dupuis, *Toward a Christian Theology of Religious Pluralism,* New York, Orbis Books, 2001, pp. 159-160; Marcello Zago, *La Nostra aetate e il Dialogo Interreligioso a ventanni dal Concilio*, Monferrato, Edizioni Piemme, 1986, p. 11.

8 Cfr. Edward P. Hahnenberg, *A Concise Guide to the Documents of Vatican II*, p. 156; Marcello Zago, *La Nostra aetate e il Dialogo Interreligioso a ventanni dal Concilio*, p. 11.

1.2.1. Essential unity of the human race

Nostra aetate places the meeting of the Church with non-Christian religions in the broad context of the common origin and common destiny of all people, and what all human beings have in common, in seeking answers to the ultimate questions of life through religion[9], and how Christians ought to act toward their brothers and sisters who do not share the Christian faith. The document insists on the essential unity of the human race, based on the fact that, all men and women have God as their creator and their ultimate Goal, and that God's saving design is extended to all peoples, and reminds Christians of their duty to foster unity and charity among individuals and nations.[10] Because of these common elements between Christians and non-Christians, and the brotherhood of all people, irrespective of their race, colour, religion and other perspectives of life, the Church urges her followers to treat others with respect and love, and avoid any form of harassment or discrimination against people, in theory or in practice.[11]

1.2.2. Deep religious sense in people

According to *Nostra aetate*, one finds in people a certain awareness of a hidden power, which lies behind the course of nature and the events of human life, and sometimes one even finds recognition of a

9 *Nostra aetate* says that, i*rrespective of their origin, people ask themselves similar profound questions, such as*: What is man? What is the meaning and purpose of life? What is upright behaviour, what is sinful? Where does suffering originate, and what end does it serve? How can genuine happiness be found? What happens at death? What is judgment? What reward follows death? What is the ultimate mystery, beyond human explanation, which embraces our entire existence, from which we take our origin and towards which we tend? Cfr. *Nostra aetate*, in *Acta Apostolicae Sedis,* 58 (1966), no. 1. (All direct citations in English from the documents of Vatican II are taken from *Vatican Council II. The Conciliar and Post-Conciliar Documents,* Austin Flannery (ed.), Bombay, St. Paul Publications, 1975).

10 Cfr. *Nostra aetate*, no. 1.

11 Cfr. Ibid., no. 5.

supreme being or, still more, a Father. This awareness and recognition results in a way of life imbued with a deep religious sense.[12]

1.2.3. Hinduism, Buddhism and other religions

Nostra aetate, mindful of the expressed desire of many Asian bishops, explicitly mentions Hinduism and Buddhism. In Hinduism people explore the divine mystery and express it both in the limitless riches of myth and the accurately defined insights of philosophy. It proposes release from the trials of the present life by ascetical practices, profound mediation, and recourse to God in confidence and love.[13] Buddhism in its various forms, testifies to the essential inadequacy of this changing world, and proposes a way of life by which people can, with confidence and trust, attain a state of perfect liberation, and reach supreme illumination, either through their own efforts or by the aid of divine help.[14] In the same way, other religions which are found throughout the world attempt in their own ways to calm the hearts of people by outlining a programme of life covering doctrine, moral precepts and sacred rites.[15] The Church's encounter with these religions should manifest deep respect for their rich traditions.

1.2.4. High regard for Muslims

The third article of *Nostra aetate* is devoted to Muslims, and points out the special links that exist between them and Christians. It says that the Church has high regard for Muslims because they worship God, who is one, living and subsistent, merciful and almighty, the creator of heaven and earth and who has spoken to human beings, and they strive to submit themselves to God as Abraham did, to whose faith Muslims eagerly link their own. Moreover, they venerate Jesus as a prophet and his Virgin Mother Mary. Because they await the day of judgment following the resurrection of the dead, they

---

12 Cfr. Ibid., no. 2.

13 Cfr. Ibid.

14 Cfr. Ibid.

15 Cfr. Ibid.

value an upright life that gives importance to worship, alms-giving and fasting. Therefore, the council asks all to forget past quarrels and to make a sincere effort at mutual understanding for the benefit of all people, and for the preservation and promotion of peace, liberty, social justice and moral values.[16]

1.2.5. Church's special relationship with Jewish people

The fourth and most extensive article of *Nostra aetate* is devoted to the relationship between Christians and the Jewish people, "the people of the New Covenant to the stock of Abraham".[17] The Church understands that, the beginning of her faith and election is to be found in the patriarchs, Moses and the prophets, and that the salvation of the Church is mystically prefigured in the exodus. She received the revelation of the Old Testament through the Jews, and draws nourishment from it. Christianity not only traces its origin to the Jewish community, into which Jesus Christ was born of a young Jewish girl of Nazareth, the Virgin Mary, but it is also built upon the apostles who were of Jewish descent, as were many of those early disciples who proclaimed the Gospel to the world.[18]

The Church recognizes with St. Paul that the Jewish people remain very dear to God, and that God does not take back the gifts he bestowed, or the choice he made (Rom 11:28-29).[19] In particular, the council affirms that neither all Jews indiscriminately at that time, nor Jews of today, can be charged with the crimes committed during the passion of Christ.[20] Moreover, although it is true that the Church is the new people of God, the Jewish people should not be spoken of as rejected or accursed as if this followed from Holy Scripture.[21] Therefore, the Church opposes every form of persecution, and

16 Cfr. Ibid. no. 3.

17 Ibid., no. 4.

18 Cfr. Ibid.

19 Cfr. Ibid.

20 Cfr. Ibid.

21 Cfr. Ibid.

deplores all anti-Semitism levelled at any time or from any source against the Jewish people.[22]

The text does not speak of the conversion of Jews to Christianity. Instead, it points to the future reign of God when all people will be one and call on Him with once voice.[23] Since the Christians and Jews have a common spiritual heritage, the council wishes to encourage and further mutual understanding, esteem, appreciation and dialogue.[24]

In order to understand better the value of these positive statements about the Jewish people, one should keep in mind the following: for many centuries, the Roman Catholic relationship to Jewish people was frequently a story of 'official' oppression and discrimination as the Church gradually considered the Jews guilty of 'deicide' ('killing' Jesus the Son of God), and consequently rejected by God. In Christian tradition, the Jewish people were also considered, with the coming of Christ, to have lost their special place as the people of God. Myths and legends that painted the Jews in a bad light grew over the centuries, and were often portrayed publicly in sculpture, painting and literature. In the Christian understanding, salvation for the Jewish people lay in conversion to Christianity.[25]

1.2.6. Recognition of positive elements in non-Christian religions

Nostra Aetate recognizes the positive elements found in non-Christian religions. The authentic moral and religious aspects found in other religions may be acceptable as means to reach salvation for the followers of those religions. Thus, for the first time, the Catholic

22 Cfr. Ibid.

23 Cfr. Ibid.

24 The relationship of the Catholic Church to the Jews is recognised as distinct from her relationship to non-Christian religions, given the unique common patrimony that Christians and Jewish people share. A special commission for religious relations with the Jews is entrusted with overseeing this relationship, and is under the care of the Pontifical Council for Promoting Christian Unity, and *not* under Pontifical Council for Interreligious Dialogue.

25 Cfr. Edward Idris Cassidy, *Ecumenism and Interreligious Dialogue,* pp. 125-126.

Church acknowledged as legitimate both the search for God by those outside the Church, and the presence of elements of truth in non-Christian religions. It also showed the Church's willingness to accept anything that is true, good and holy in other religions. The document made a very significant statement, affirming this: "The Catholic Church rejects nothing of what is true and holy in these religions. She has a high regard for the manner of life and conduct, the precepts and doctrines which, although differing in many ways from her own teaching, nevertheless, often reflect a ray of that Truth [*radium illius Veritatis*] which enlightens all men."[26] It then added: "Let Christians, [...] acknowledge, preserve and encourage the spiritual and moral truths found among non-Christians, also their social life and culture."[27]

1.2.7. Fraternal treatment, dialogue and collaboration

The concluding section of *Nostra aetate* declares that it is impossible to truly pray to God the Father of all, if anyone treats any person in other than brotherly or sisterly fashion, for all people are created in God's image. It condemns, both in theory and practice, any form of discrimination against people or harassment of them on the basis of their race, colour, condition in life or religion, for such discrimination violates human dignity and human rights.[28] It exhorts all Christians to be at peace with all, and engage in dialogue and collaboration with the followers of other religions with prudence and charity, and bearing witness to Christian faith and life.[29]

1.2.8. Church is duty-bound to proclaim Jesus Christ

Nostra aetate affirms that, the Church has always held, and continues to hold, that Christ is the way, the truth and the life (Jn 4:6), and that he, out of infinite love, freely underwent suffering and death so

26 *Nostra aetate*, no. 2.

27 Ibid.

28 Cfr. Ibid., no. 5.

29 Cfr. Ibid., nos. 2, 5.

that all might attain salvation and find fullness of their religious life. Therefore, it is the duty of the Church to proclaim Christ as the sign of God's universal love and the source of all grace.[30] This means that the Church's positive attitude towards non-Christian religions does not in any way diminish her missionary zeal.

1.3 Pastoral approach of *Nostra aetate*

Nostra aetate is basically a pastoral document, and not meant as a theological treatise. It is simple, concrete and practical, and exhorts all people to overcome divisions and foster friendly relations. Such a relationship should be based on what all people – their specific religious allegiances notwithstanding – have in common. The ancient prejudices and negative assessments have to be destroyed through mutual appreciation, dialogue and collaboration, and by pointing to positive values and divine endowments contained in other religions.[31]

1.4 Influence of *Nostra aetate*

Prior to *Nostra aetate*, non-Christian religions were often considered 'pagan', 'false' or even the fruit of Satan's presence in the world. Christian missionary apostolate was primarily addressed to them, or to people of more 'primitive' spiritual beliefs, in the hope of saving the souls of their followers. Dialogue with these religions was rare and directed principally at conversion. Some Christian scholars came to appreciate the positive contribution that these great religions made to the spiritualty of their followers, but their work was often looked upon, officially, with scepticism and concern.[32] But with *Nostra aetate* the context changed radically. The document expresses the existence of authentic values in non-Christian religions more forcefully than any of the previous documents of the Catholic Church. In other religions there is the real presence of 'that Truth' – though incomplete

30 Cfr. Ibid., nos. 2, 4.

31 Cfr. Jacques Dupuis, *Toward a Christian Theology of Religious Pluralism,* p. 160.

32 Cfr. Edward Idris Cassidy, *Ecumenism and Interreligious Dialogue,* p. 126.

and in the form of 'ray'. This is the foundation for the Church's respect towards them and for her wish to promote their spiritual and cultural values. Nevertheless, the Church's mission requires that it proclaims the fullness of Truth in Jesus Christ.[33]

2. Non-Christian religions in the other documents of Vatican II

Besides *Nostra aetate* there are also other conciliar documents that discuss non-Christian religions, especially *Lumen gentium* (*LG*; Dogmatic Constitution on the Church, 21 November 1964); *Ad gentes* (*AG*; Decree on the Church's Missionary Activity, 7 December 1965); *Gaudium et spes* (*GS*; Pastoral Constitution on the Church in the Modern World, 7 December 1965) and *Dignitatis humanae* (*DH*; Declaration on Religious Liberty, 7 December 1965). In addition, there are documents that deal with non-Christian religions indirectly or in passing, such as: *Dei verbum* (*DV*; Dogmatic Constitution on Divine Revelation, 18 November 1965); *Apostolicam actuositatem* (*AA*; Decree on the Apostolate of the Laity, 18 November 1965); *Presbyterorum ordnis* (*PO*; Decree on the Ministry and Life of Priests, 7 December 1965); *Optatam totius* (*OT*; Decree on the Training of Priests, 28 October 1965); *Christus Dominus* (*CD*; Decree on the Pastoral Office of Bishops in the Church, 28 October 1965); *Sacrosanctum concilium* (*SC*; The Constitution on the Sacred Liturgy, 4 December 1963), etc. We shall analyse them briefly.

2.1 *Lumen gentium*

The Dogmatic Constitution *Lumen gentium* ('Light of the Nations) is one of the principal documents of Vatican II. When considering the non-Christians, it first discusses the Jewish people. It states that they are that people to which the covenants and promises were made, and from which Christ was born according to the flesh (Rom 9:4-5). In view of the divine choice, they are a people most dear for the sake of the fathers, and, while the Jews do not recognise in Christ the promised Messiah, God has not withdrawn his covenant with

33 Cfr. Jacques Dupuis, *Toward a Christian Theology of Religious Pluralism*, p. 164.

them (Rom 11:28-29).[34] The document next considers the Muslims as people who acknowledge the creator and profess to hold the faith of Abraham, and who, together with the Christians, adore the one, merciful God, who will judge humanity on the last day.[35] The document does not refer directly to any other religion by name, but alludes to them broadly when it says that God is not remote from those who in shadows and images seek the unknown God, since he gives to all people life and breath and all things (Acts 17:25-28), and since he wills all people to be saved (1Tim 2:4).[36]

Another important affirmation of *Lumen gentium* is that all people are called by God's grace to salvation,[37] and that the *possibility* of salvation exists also outside the visible Church, for those people, through no fault of their own, have not known the Gospel of Christ or the Church, provided they direct their life according to the dictates of their conscience. It also states that all those who seek God with a sincere heart or strive to lead a good life do so because they are moved by God's grace. The document says: "Those who, through no fault of their own, do not know the Gospel of Christ or his Church, but who nevertheless seek God with a sincere heart, and, moved by grace, try in their actions to do his will as they know it through the dictates of their conscience – those too may achieve eternal salvation."[38] In spite of this, Christ's command to preach the Gospel to every creature (Mk 16:16) remains mandatory for the Church.[39]

The document also declares that, whatever good or truth is found among non-Christian religions is considered by the Church as a preparation for the Gospel (*praeparatio evangelica*).[40] It further

34 Cfr. *Lumen gentium,* in *Acta Apostolicae Sedis,* 57 (1965), no. 16.

35 Cfr. Ibid.

36 Cfr. Ibid.

37 Cfr. Ibid., no. 13.

38 Ibid., no. 16.

39 Cfr. Ibid.

40 Cfr. Ibid. The expression 'preparation for the Gospel' is an idea taken from Bishop Eusebius of Caesarea. Cfr. Jacques Dupuis, *Toward a Christian Theology of Religious Pluralism,* p. 162.

says that whatever good is found sown in the minds and hearts of people or in their rites, abilities, resources and customs, is not only preserved from destruction, but also purified, strengthened, elevated, and perfected for the glory of God and the happiness of persons.[41]

Jacques Dupuis calls our attention to the inverse order in which the relations of the Church to non-Christian religions are proposed in *Lumen gentium* 16 and in *Nostra aetate* 2-4. *Lumen gentium* first discusses the Jews, then the Muslims and then all other non-Christians. *Nostra aetate* follows the reverse order: human religiosity in general; the religions which are found in more advanced civilisations, such as, Hinduism, Buddhism and others; Islam, and finally Judaism.[42]

2.2 *Ad gentes*

The Decree *Ad gentes* ('To the nations') has several passages that explain the function of the Church's missionary activity in relation to non-Christian religions. In the first place, the document acknowledges that there are large groups of people who belong to one or other of the great religions of the world.[43] The non-Christians are related to the people of God because the Holy Spirit was at work in the world before Christ was glorified.[44] Many people seek God through religions in their attempt to touch him and find him, although God is not far from any of us (Acts 17:27).[45] But their efforts need to be enlightened and corrected, so that these religions may lead one to the true God, and be a preparation for the Gospel.[46]

The Church's missionary activity recognises the goodness in the non-Christian world. It purifies, elevates, and brings to perfection in Christ the truth, grace and goodness which are already found sown in the hearts and minds of human beings or in their customs, cultures

41 Cfr. *Lumen gentium*, nos. 13, 17.

42 Cfr. Jacques Dupuis, *Toward a Christian Theology of Religious Pluralism*, p. 160.

43 Cfr. *Ad gentes*, in *Acta Apostolicae Sedis*, 58 (1966), no. 10.

44 Cfr. Ibid., no. 4.

45 Cfr. Ibid.. no. 3.

46 Cfr. Ibid., no. 3.

and traditions, and which are, as it were, a secret presence of God.[47] In order to be able to witness to Christ fruitfully, Christians must be familiar with their national and religious traditions, and with joy and respect, they must discover the seeds of the Word (*semina Verbi*) hidden among them.[48]

Through sincere and patient dialogue with other religions, Christians can learn what treasures God has distributed among the nations.[49] They should be eager to collaborate in projects initiated by private, public, state or international bodies, or by other Christians, or even by non-Christian religions.[50] In priestly formation the students should be properly prepared for fraternal dialogue with non-Christians.[51] In philosophy and theology they should examine the relationship between the traditions and religions of their homeland and Christianity.[52] All missionaries – priests, religious, sisters and laity – should be trained and formed, each according to their state, and be instructed, so that they might have a general knowledge of peoples, cultures and religions.[53] Christian charity is extended to all without distinction of race, social condition or religion.[54] Finally, in ways known to himself, God can lead those who, through no fault of their own, are ignorant of the Gospel to that faith without which it is impossible to please him. The Church, nevertheless, has the obligation and the sacred right to evangelise. Consequently, missionary activity, directed towards non-Christians, retains at all times its full force and necessity.[55]

---

47 Cfr. Ibid., no. 9.

48 Cfr. Ibid., no. 11.

49 Cfr. Ibid.

50 Cfr. Ibid., no. 12.

51 Cfr. Ibid., no. 16.

52 Cfr. Ibid.

53 Cfr. Ibid., no. 26.

54 Cfr. Ibid., no. 12.

55 Cfr. Ibid., no. 7.

2.3 *Gaudium et spes*

The Pastoral Constitution *Gaudium ete spes* ('Joy and hope') acknowledges that, divine grace is active invisibly in the hearts of all people of good will[56] – this naturally includes also non-Christians. It further states that, since Christ died for all, the Holy Spirit offers to all people, in ways known to God, the possibility of being made partners in the paschal mystery of Christ.[57] Another significant affirmation is that, the Spirit of God is powerfully and universally at work in the world, which is evident not only in the religious aspirations of human beings but also in the human values they pursue, such as brotherhood, charity, truth, freedom, peace, unity, harmony, service, dialogue, co-operation, etc.[58] The document says: "[…] man is continually being aroused by the Spirit of God and that he will never be utterly indifferent to religion. – a fact confirmed by the experience of ages past and plentiful evidence at the present day";[59] "It is by the gift of the Holy Spirit that man, through faith, comes to contemplate and savour the mystery of God's designs."[60]

There are statements in the same document which *indirectly affirm* the value of non-Christian religions. For instance, it understands culture as something positive, and practising religion as part of it.[61] It states that the Church wishes to preserve the precious religious and human elements found in traditions that believe in God;[62] it speaks of tolerance of others who differ in religion, and criticises political systems that hinder religious liberty;[63] it expresses happiness in seeing the spirit of true brotherhood existing between Christians

---

56 Cfr. *Gaudium et spes,* in *Acta Apostolicae Sedis,* 58 (1966), no. 22.

57 Cfr. Ibid.

58 Cfr. Ibid., no. 92.

59 Ibid., no. 41.

60 Ibid., no. 15.

61 Cfr. Ibid., no. 53.

62 Cfr. Ibid., no. 92.

63 Cfr. Ibid., no. 73.

and non-Christians, and wishes to intensify its collaboration with them in alleviating human misery.[64]

2.4 *Dignitatis humanae*

The Declaration *Dignitatis humanae* ('Of the Dignity of the Human Person') begins by stating that the demand for freedom in human society is concerned chiefly with the spiritual values of people, especially with what concerns the free practice of religion in society.[65] None should deny free existence of religion in society, when the just requirements of public order are observed.[66] The document strongly affirms freedom of conscience, and declares that the right to religious freedom is based on the very dignity of the human person.[67] It also means that, all people are immune from coercion on the part of individuals, social groups and every human power so that, within due limits, nobody is forced to act against his or her convictions in religious matters, in private or in public, alone or in association with others.[68]

Religious communities are a requirement of the nature of human beings, and of religion itself, and they have the right not to be prevented from publically teaching and bearing witness to their beliefs by the spoken or written word. Religious groups are not to be prevented from freely demonstrating the special value of their teaching, to hold meetings or establish educational, cultural,

---

64 Cfr. Ibid., no. 84.

65 Cfr. *Dignitatis humanae*, in *Acta Apostolicae Sedis,* 58 (1966), no. 1.

66 Cfr. Ibid., no. 3.

67 Cfr. Ibid., nos. 2, 12. Prior to Vatican II, there were recurring condemnation of 'freedom of conscience and of worship' as 'insanity' by Gregory XVI, and Pius IX was convinced that civil freedom of cult leads to religious indifferentism. Cfr. Laurent Cleenewerck, *His Broken Body. Understanding and Healing the Schism between the Roman Catholic and Eastern Orthodox Churches (An Orthodox Perspective),* Washington, Euclid University Consortium Press, 2007, p. 47; *The Christian Faith in the Doctrinal Documents of the Catholic Church*, J. Neuner and J. Dupuis (eds.), Bangalore, Theological Publications, 1982, pp. 280, 283-284.

68 Cfr. *Dignitatis humanae*, no. 2.

charitable and social organisations, prompted by their own religious sense.[69]

Another important affirmation of the document is that, every human being is obliged to follow their conscience faithfully, especially in religious matters.[70] Though the text affirms that the one true religion subsists in the Catholic and Apostolic Church,[71] it also states that, nobody is to be forced to embrace the faith against one's will.[72] People must be allowed to honour the supreme Godhead with public worship, help their members to practice their religion, strengthen them with religious instruction, and promote institutions in which members may work together to organise their own lives according to their religious principles.[73] Families have the right freely to organise their own religious life and to decide in accordance with their own religious beliefs, the form of religious upbringing which is to be given to their children.[74]

The civil authority must protect religious freedom and help to create conditions favourable to the fostering of religious life so that, the citizens will be really in a position to exercise their religious rights and fulfil their religious duties.[75] To establish and strengthen peaceful relations and harmony in the human race, religious freedom must be given effective constitutional protection.[76] Therefore, the civil authority must recognise and look with favour on the religious life of the citizens, and should not attempt to control or restrict religious activity, lest it should overstep the limits of its power.[77]

---

69 Cfr. Ibid., 4.

70 Cfr. Ibid., no. 3.

71 Cfr. Ibid., no. 1. The text in Latin reads: "*Hanc unicam veram Religionem subsistere eredimus in catholica et apostolica Ecclesia*".

72 Cfr. Ibid., no. 10.

73 Cfr. Ibid., no. 4.

74 Cfr. Ibid., no. 5.

75 Cfr. Ibid., no. 6.

76 Cfr. Ibid., no. 15.

77 Cfr. Ibid., no. 3.

2.5 Some minor references to non-Christian religions

There are also brief references to non-Christian religions, either direct or indirect, in some of the other documents of Vatican II. For example, the Decree on the Apostolate of the Lay People (*Apostolicam actuositatem*, 'Apostolic Activity'), after emphasizing the importance of Catholic lay persons collaborating with other Christians, speaks also of the need to co-operate with those who do not profess the Christian religion (an obvious reference, first of all, to non-Christians), because they too acknowledge the human values that are common to human beings.[78]

In the Constitution on the Sacred Liturgy (*Sacrosanctum concilium,* 'Sacred Council') one can find an indirect reference to other religions when it asks Christians to respect and foster, and even adapt in liturgy, things that are good and true, found among the various races and peoples, provided they are not indissolubly bound up with superstition and error.[79]

The Decree on the Training of Priests (*Optatam totius)* states that students are to be introduced to the knowledge of whatever other religions are most commonly encountered in their region, so that they may recognise more clearly how much goodness and truth they possess through the Providence of God, and learn how to refute their errors, and bring the light of truth to those who are without it.[80]

In the Decree on the Pastoral Office of Bishops in the Church (*Christus Dominus*, 'Christ the Lord'), the bishops are asked to manifest solicitude also towards the non-baptised (i.e. non-Christians), so that the charity of Christ may shine on them too, of whom bishops are the witnesses before all people.[81]

In the Dogmatic Constitution on Divine Revelation (*Dei verbum*, 'Word of God'), no direct mention is made of non-Christian religions. But it states that, people can come to know God

78 Cfr. *Apostolicam actuositatem*, in *Acta Apostolicae Sedis*, 58 (1966), no. 27.

79 Cfr. *Sacrosanctum concilium*, in *Acta Apostolicae Sedis,* 56 (1964), no. 37.

80 Cfr. *Optatam totius*, in *Acta Apostolicae Sedis,* 58 (1966), no.16.

81 Cfr. *Christus Dominus*, in *Acta Apostolicae Sedis,* 58 (1966), no. 16.

by reflecting on the created world (Rom 1:20).[82] The document does not say that non-Christian scriptures are inspired. Yet some openness towards other religions is manifested when it says that, editions of Sacred Scriptures, with suitable notes, should be prepared for the use of even non-Christians, and adapted to their circumstances.[83]

Thus, references to non-Christian religions are abundant in the documents of the Vatican II. While in some the statements are direct, in others they are indirect. The overall approach is more pastoral than theological, and its objective is to promote mutual appreciation, respect, dialogue and collaboration.

3. Theological foundations for affirming non-Christian religions

In the documents of Vatican II analysed above, we have come across many references to the theological foundations for affirming the value of non-Christian religions. Though they are scattered in many documents, they may be summed up thus: the Catholic Church rejects nothing of what is true and holy in other religions (*NA* 2); the Holy Spirit offers to all the possibility of being made partners in the paschal mystery of Christ (*GS* 22); divine grace is active invisibly in the hearts of all people of good will (*GS* 22); *all of humankind is called by God's grace to salvation (LG 13,16);* elements that are true and good are found in other religions (*LG* 16); non-Christian religions often reflect a 'ray of that Truth' which illumines all humankind (*NA* 2); other religions contain 'true and good things' (*OT* 16), 'precious things, both religious and human' (*GS* 92), 'seeds of contemplation' (*AG* 18), 'seeds of the Word' (*AG* 11,15), 'elements of truth and grace' (*AG* 9); non-Christian religions manifest 'a secret presence of God' (*AG* 9), and are 'a preparation for the Gospel' (*LG* 16; *AG* 3).

82 Cfr. *Dei verbum*, nos. 3, 6.

83 Cfr. Ibid., no. 25.

4. Theological and pastoral implications of the teachings of Vatican II

The teachings of Vatican II on non-Christian religions have far-reaching consequences for Catholic theology of religion and pastoral action. It also affects the general perception of other religions, and the manner in which interactions are carried out with them. We shall briefly analyse some of them.

4.1 Non-Christian religions provide basis for relationship with God

Vatican II acknowledges that religions of the world fulfil many valuable functions for their followers. They have transmitted, and continue to transmit, treasures of wisdom, religiosity and spiritual insights, and thereby sustain the human and spiritual journey of people. Through them, human beings establish a relationship with God or the Transcendent or the Absolute, find resources for moral life, and nurture hope for life after death, liberation or salvation. Thus, they realise and develop that natural openness to the Transcendent, which is common to every human being, and constitute the foundation of their religious attitude and behaviour.

4.2 Possibility of salvation for non-Christians

Vatican II affirms the *possibility* of salvation for non-Christians.[84] This means that, the activity of God's salvific grace is *not restricted to*

84 Cfr. *Lumen gentium*, no. 16; *Gaudium et spes*, 22. This was an amazing statement from a Church which had believed for many centuries that, there was 'no salvation outside the Church' (*extra ecclesiam nulla salus*). It may be recalled here that, the Fourth Lateran Council (1215) repeated Bishop Cyprian's formula, *extra ecclesiam nulla salus* (obviously, taking it out of the original context of schism in the Church, and interpreting it literally). The Council of Florence (1442) upheld the same view, and assumed a more rigid understanding of the axiom. A century later (1547), the Council of Trent with a doctrine of 'baptism of desire' solemnly affirmed the possibility of salvation for those who were outside the Church. The later Church documents reaffirmed, though not without a marked caution, such a *possibility*. But over the centuries, hardly ever did Church documents, whether conciliar or otherwise, take a position on religions as such, let alone any positive manner. Cfr. Paul F. Knitter, *No Other Name? A Critical Survey of Christian Attitudes Towards the*

the visible boundaries of the Church. It may be recalled here that, prior to Vatican II, the famous 8 August 1949 letter from the Holy Office to the Archbishop of Boston underscored the Church's position that there was no salvation outside the Church, and that it was among the truths the Church had always taught. But it is not always required that a person be incorporated into the Church *actually* as a member, in order to be saved; it is sufficient that one is at least united to her by desire and longing, even implicitly.[85] This means that, to be saved, one need not necessarily follow the Gospel by being a member of the *visible* Church. This was in sharp contrast to what the ecumenical council of Florence solemnly declared in 1442:

> [The holy Roman Church] firmly believes, professes and preaches that "no one remaining outside the Catholic Church, not only pagans", but also Jews, heretics or schismatics, can become partakers of eternal life; but they will go to the "eternal fire prepared for the devil and his angels" *(Mt. 25, 41),* unless before the end of their life they are received into it. For union with the body of the Church is of so great importance that the sacraments of the Church are helpful to salvation only for those remaining in it; and fasts, almsgiving, other works of piety, and the exercises of a militant Christian life bear eternal rewards for them alone. "And no one can be saved, no matter how much alms he has given, even if he sheds his blood for the name of Christ, unless he remains in the bosom and unity of the Catholic Church".[86]

World Religions, London, SCM Press, 1985, p. 122; Jacques Dupuis, *Christianity and the Religions. From Confrontation to Dialogue*, Philip Berryman (tr.), New York, Orbis Books, 2002, pp. 59-60.

85 Cfr. *The Christian Faith in the Doctrinal Documents of the Catholic Church*, J. Neuner and J. Dupuis (eds.), pp. 240-242.

86 Ibid., pp. 222-223.

The new teaching of Vatican II, in a way, 'contradicts' the above-mentioned position of the Church.[87] According to the new teaching, what one needs is not to deny deliberately the Gospel or refuse to enter into the Church, indicating thereby that it is not the truth.[88] But the *salvation of non-Christians comes not from their own religion but through Christ and the Church.* It can be concluded, therefore, that although the Church acknowledges the possibility of salvation for non-Christians, it does not recognise that their own religions are ways of salvation for them.

4.3 All are saved by Christ and in his Church

Basing itself on Scripture and tradition, Vatican II teaches that the Church is necessary for salvation, that Christ is the only mediator[89] and the way of salvation, and that he is present in his body, which is the Church.[90] But, as we have already seen, it also states that, those who, through no fault of their own, do not know the Gospel of Christ or his Church, but who nevertheless are sincerely searching for God, and, under the influence of grace, trying their best, through good works, to fulfil God's will made known to them through the dictates of their conscience, can achieve eternal salvation.[91] This implies two things: first, that *all salvation is through Christ* even though non-Christians may not be aware of it; second, that even those who do not actually belong to the visible Church are objectively oriented towards it, as they are *part of that wider, invisible Church,* known only to God. As a consequence of this, according to Karl Rahner, Christians will regard the non-Christians not as having no part in Christianity or as standing altogether outside salvation because they

87 But the 'contradiction' definitely has a very positive impact on both ecumenical and interreligious dialogues.

88 Cfr. *Lumen gentium*, no. 14.

89 Cfr. Ibid. "For there is one God and one Mediator between God and man, himself a man, Jesus Christ, who gave himself as a ransom for all." (1 Tim 2:4-5). See also *Ad gentes*, nos. 3, 7.

90 Cfr. *Lumen gentium*, no. 14.

91 Cfr. Ibid., no. 16.

are not Christians, but rather as 'anonymous Christians' who do not realise what they truly are in virtue of grace in the depth of their consciousness.[92]

4.4 Commitment to dialogue and collaboration

The documents of Vatican II are very much pastoral in nature. They exhort the members of the Church to enter into dialogue (*colloquia*) and collaboration (*collaboratio*) with the followers of other religions. But these activities have to be carried out with prudence and charity, and in witness to the Christian faith and life. Therefore, Christians are asked to respect religious liberty and freedom of conscience, recognise, preserve and promote those true and good things, spiritual and moral, as well as the human, social and cultural values found among other religions. Rather than looking for errors and condemning what is found in them as incompatible with Christian teaching, dialogue and co-operation are proposed in order to promote, peace, justice, unity, brotherhood, harmony and advancement of the human community. In this way, Vatican II paved the way for fruitful interreligious dialogue and collaboration with non-Christian religions. In 1964 Pope Paul VI instituted, as an institutional sign of the Church's desire to meet and relate to the followers of other religions of the world, the Secretariat for Non-Christians, an organism distinct from the Sacred Congregation for the Evangelisation of Peoples.

But it may be recalled that 'dialogue' was not a concept that one could easily trace in the draft documents of Vatican II prepared by the preparatory commissions. But later, it became the 'spirit' of the council. On 6 August 1964, Pope Paul VI issued his first encyclical *Ecclesiam suam.* As already said, it had a direct impact on Vatican II in one important regard, namely, the remarkable prominence it gives to dialogue. Dialogue occurs in it seventy-seven times, and

92 Cfr. Karl Rahner, *Theological Investigations*, Vol. 10. *Writings of 1965-1967 (2)*, David Bourke (tr.), London, Darton, Longman and Todd, 1973, p. 16. Rahner' concept of 'anonymous Christians' has been severely criticised by many theologians.

its meaning and application occupy fully two-thirds of this long document. It may be rightly noted that the original version of the document on ecumenism, presented to the council the previous year, the word 'dialogue' did not appear a single time. In its revised version presented after the publication of the encyclical, it became one of the text's most characteristic words. Thus, 'dialogue' became the typical spirit of Vatican II, and it made its way into the council's vocabulary, and it is reflected in many of the documents it produced.[93]

4.5 The need to correct and purify distortions and errors

Although the non-Christian religions contain many things that are true and good, the documents of Vatican II also state that one should never forget nor overlook the fact that, they also contain false elements, distortions, incomplete truths as well as theoretical and practical errors. Hence, the values they present must be tested in the light of Christian revelation; in accepting the truth they contain, one should examine if they are compatible with the Christian faith; and whatever is false or distorted must be purified and corrected.

4.6 Church is duty-bound to proclaim Christ

Though there is optimism about the possibility of salvation for people belonging to other religions, and about dialogue and collaboration with those religions, Vatican II does not make the call to proclaim Christ and the Gospel any less urgent. In addition, it clearly teaches that there is only one mediator between human beings and God, Jesus Christ, implying thereby that all salvation is through Christ and his Church. Hence, the Church is duty-bound to proclaim Christ, who is the way, the truth and the life (Jn 14:6), so that people may find the fullness of their religious life.[94]

---

93 Cfr. John W. O'Malley, *What Happened at Vatican II*, pp. 203-204.

94 Cfr. *Nostra aetate*, no. 2. At the time of the promulgation of the *Nostra aetate*, there were some conservative bishops in the Vatican council who opposed it by arguing that, the document would lead to indifference to the Church's missionary

4.7 Birth of Catholic theology of religions

Vatican II laid the solid foundation for a Catholic theology of religions. According to Jacques Dupuis, Catholic theology of religion came to be born around the time of Vatican II, that is, during the years which directly prepared for it, and those that followed. In the 1960s, the possibility of a positive role played by other religions for the salvation of their members became an object of theological reflection in its own right.[95]

Dupuis traces three periods in the development of Catholic theology of religions. The first period belongs to the first quarter of the twentieth century, and it was dominated by an *apologetic* attitude, mostly negative. The middle of the century, and the years leading to and immediately following Vatican II, witnessed a gradual change of climate to which the council gave a powerful impetus. During this second period, the approach became less defensive and more *positive.* In the wake of the council, other religions were progressively considered as containing positive values or even as playing a positive role in the salvation of their members. According to Dupuis, with this new attitude, the Catholic theology of religions was born. The third period is traced to the beginning of the 1980s that was marked by a broader perspective, and it gave birth to a 'theology of religious pluralism'. Going beyond the problematic of people's salvation in and through their religious traditions, the new perspective seeks to penetrate more deeply into God's plan for humankind. [96]

Over the past decades, the theological position with regard to non-Christian religions has taken three major directions among the

---

activity, and even put an end to it by regarding all religions as of the same value. But this explicit call for proclamation of Christ clarifies the stand of the Church.

95 Cfr. Jacques Dupuis, *Toward a Christian Theology of Religious Pluralism,* p. 2.

96 Cfr. Ibid., pp. 12-13.

Roman Catholic theologians, namely the exclusivist[97], inclusivist[98], and pluralist.[99] A fourth approach avoids the issue of salvation altogether, emphasizing instead the need for dialogue and mutual understanding.[100]

5. A critical appreciation

Vatican II presents a very positive attitude towards non-Christian religions, manifested in its openness and appreciation, and willingness to enter into dialogue and collaboration with them. The documents produced by it recognise, in other religions, the presence of holiness and truth, and even the possibility of salvation for their followers. This was a revolutionary and positive development in the official position of the Catholic Church, which until then had often considered the non-Christian religions as 'error', 'falsity', 'superstition' and 'idolatry', with the consequent negative attitude of disregard and rejection.

When the Church affirms that the non-Christian religions are 'a preparation for the Gospel', it is implied that they, rather than being an obstacle to Christian faith, have played a positive role before the Christ-event. They are not obsolete with the Christ-event, because they continue to assume the same role of 'a preparation for

---

97 The *exclusivist* position interprets Christ's words literally: "No one comes to the Father except through me" (Jn 14:6). This means that, salvation is granted by Christ in and through the Church alone; other religions are false and misleading. This viewpoint was held by many Catholics up until Vatican II, but it was clearly set aside by the Council. Cfr. Edward P. Hahnenberg, *A Concise Guide to the Documents of Vatican II*, p. 162.

98 The *inclusivist* position holds that Christ may also work through other religions in a hidden way. When people of any religion strive to live a good life, and try to do the will of God, or follow their conscience, they are in fact being guided by Christ, even if they do not know it. This position tries to balance the belief that Christ is the one unique saviour of the world alongside the possibility of salvation for the good people of other religions. It is the position closest to the Roman Catholic Church's official teaching today. Cfr. Ibid., p. 162.

99 The *pluralist* position argues that Christ is an important saviour, but not the only one. Figures in other religions, such as the Buddha and Krishna, also offer salvation for their followers. Cfr. Ibid., p. 162.

100 Cfr. Ibid., p. 162.

the Gospel', until such time as the Gospel would be *existentially proclaimed, and the fullness of truth in Jesus Christ is revealed to all.* This means that, the non-Christian religions continue to play a positive role in the world even now, and, consequently, Christianity cannot exclude other religions. But at the same time, a difference of degree between non-Christian religions and Christianity is implied here, inasmuch as Christianity contains in a complete and perfect form what remains fragmentary and imperfect in non-Christian religions.[101] This points to the uniqueness of Christianity.

If the non-Christian religions are 'a preparation for the Gospel', 'contain ray of truth', 'elements of truth and grace', and 'seeds of the Word', no religion is purely natural. Every religion is, in some way, a divine intervention in the history of the nations, and an existential mediation of the mystery of salvation in Jesus Christ. As Jacques Dupuis has rightly said, all religions, then, for more than one reason, are supernatural.[102]

Because of the positive attitude of the Church towards non-Christian religions, some question the relevance and necessity of missionary activity. But Vatican II clearly states that the possibility of salivation for the followers of non-Christian religions, positive appreciation of these faiths, and engagement in inter-religious dialogue do not do away with mission *ad gentes*. In fact, if non-Christian religions are "a preparation for the Gospel", they truly enhance missionary work.

In *Dei verbum*, nothing is said whether the non-Christian scriptures are revealed or not. It speaks only of the Old and New Testaments as inspired by God. But some other documents of Vatican II affirm that other religions reflect 'a ray of that Truth which

---

101 Cfr. Johannes B. Lotz, "Christianity and the Non-Christian Religions in their Relationship to Religious Experience", in *Vatican II Assessment and Perspectives Twenty-five Years after (1962-1987),* Vol. 3, New York, Paulist Press, 1989, p. 162. Lotz also adds that this is to be understood as concerns the *material content*, not as concerns the degree to which it is carried out, for non-Christians are very often superior to Christians in their fidelity and zeal. Cfr. Ibid.

102 Cfr. Jacques Dupuis, *Toward a Christian Theology of Religious Pluralism,* pp. 132-133.

enlightens all people'. This leads us to ask: if other religions contain a 'ray of truth', and if all truth comes ultimately from God, then should we not acknowledge that God is at work in these religions? Are not the sacred scriptures of other religions in some way inspired? Some argue that if we grant that non-Christian scriptures are also inspired, it would undermine the unique inspired character of the Bible.[103] Nevertheless, one may hold that Vatican II *implicitly* accepts the possibility of revelation in the scriptures of other religions, but they might also contain errors and incomplete truths.

Nostra aetate pays direct attention only to some of the non-Christian world religions, namely Hinduism, Buddhism, Islam and Judaism, leaving out other great religions like Confucianism, Taoism, Shintoism, Sikhism, Jainism, etc. In addition, no mention is made of the 'traditional religions' of Africa, the Americas, Asia, Oceania, etc. The document gives much importance to Judaism, and it is understandable as Judaism is paradigmatic for Christianity. But another paragraph should have been added in order to accommodate some of the other world religions. It is also to be noted that the document's description of Hinduism and Buddhism is very generic and quite elementary.

When Vatican II speaks about dialogue, one notices an implicit priority given to Judaism and Islam. While this may have been a theological and existential priority for the Western Church at the time of Vatican II, there are also 'contextual priorities' in dialogue. For the Christians of Europe and the Americas, dialogue with Jews and Muslims may be very important. But, for those of much of Asia and Africa, it is equally important to dialogue also with such religions as Hinduism, Buddhism, Confucianism, Taoism, Shintoism, Sikhism, Jainism, traditional religions, etc. Thus, the priority in dialogue proposed by the Vatican II may not be fully applicable in those parts of the world where there are very few Jews and Muslims, or where

103 Cfr. Edward P. Hahnenberg, *A Concise Guide to the Documents of Vatican II*, p. 34.

there are also other religions that are equally or more important than Judaism and Islam.[104]

Though Vatican II encourages dialogue with non-Christians, there are problems connected with it. The meaning of the term 'dialogue' needs to be better clarified. Jacques Dupuis asks the following questions: Is interreligious dialogue an intrinsic dimension of the Church's mission? Is it a matter of pre-evangelisation or evangelisation proper? Is it an end in itself, or does it represent a means ordained to the proclamation of the Gospel?[105] If the Church insists that Christ is the universal sacrament of salvation and the only mediator, Judaism, Islam and Christianity will have very little in common. It also calls into question the salvific value of non-Christian religions and the saviour figures found in them. Even though Judaism, Islam and Christianity are monotheistic religions, it is problematic if they formally worship the same God. Vatican II nowhere mentions Muhammad as a prophet, and Christianity can in no way accept him as a prophet in a formal way.[106] Some non-Christians might think that dialogue is a new and subtle from of

---

104 The emphasis placed on dialogue with Jews and Muslims is understandable. Most of the "protagonists" of the Vatican II were theologians and bishops hailing from Europe and North America, whose experience with non-Christian religions was limited, by and large, to Judaism and Islam, and the voices of the Asian and African bishops were heard in the council only in a limited way. John W. O'Malley in his book *What Happened at Vatican II* has a section with the title "Council Participants Frequently Mentioned", in which he briefly describes 62 persons who played a significant role in the Vatican II. In this list, the vast majority are from Europe and North America, and no Asian or African bishop or theologian is mentioned in it, except for a Syrian cardinal, whose experience with non-Christian religions was also limited basically to Islam and Judaism. Cfr. John W. O'Malley, *What Happened at Vatican II*, pp. 321-328.

105 Cfr. Jacques Dupuis, "Interreligious Dialogue in the Church's Evangelizing Mission. Twenty years of Evolution of a Theological Concept", in *Vatican II Assessment and Perspectives Twenty-five Years after (1962-1987)*, Vol. 3, New York, Paulist Press, 1989, p. 237.

106 For Christianity, Jesus Christ is the fullness of God's revelation (cf. Heb 1:1-4), and after him there is no formal revelation or formal prophet or formal prophecy.

evangelisation introduced by the Church.[107] On the one hand, the Church affirms the possibility of salvation also for followers of other religions. On the other hand, it stresses the necessity of evangelisation of non-Christians. All these can lead to theological conflicts, tensions, suspicion and unwillingness to dialogue, making dialogue difficult. But one should also keep in mind that interreligious dialogue does not mean discovering only the agreements between religions but also the differences

In spite of these problems, the greatest contribution of Vatican II consists in the attitudinal change it brought about in the Catholic Church. According to Jacques Dupuis, the spectrum of the Church's attitudes has moved the whole way from the dialectical *opposition* inherited from a long past, through an attitude of *tolerance*, to the *dialogical conversation* of recent years. In a parallel fashion, the theological evaluation has gone all the way from the *disregard and rejection* which characterised much of the Christian tradition, through a guarded *acceptance* and openness, to a *positive* assessment and the recognition of positive values.[108]

6. Conclusion

It is widely acknowledged that the teachings of Vatican II display an openness towards non-Christian religions, unprecedented in previous official documents of the Catholic Church. It made a positive evaluation of other religions, gave impetus to new pastoral trends, laid firm foundations for interreligious dialogue and Catholic theology of religions. Thus, Vatican II marked a true break with the past, and inaugurated a new beginning with regard to the Church's relations to other religions. According to Karl Rahner, the Church became

107 Cfr. Mariasusai Dhavamony, "Evangelisation and Dialogue in Vatican II", in *Vatican II Assessment and Perspectives Twenty-five Years after (1962-1987)*, Vol. 3, New York, Paulist Press, 1989, p. 273.

108 Cfr. Jacques Dupuis, *Toward a Christian Theology of Religious Pluralism*, p. 12.

a truly world-Church, for the first time, as a result of Vatican II.[109] Paul Knitter commenting on the attitude of the Catholic Church towards non-Christian religions says: "It might come as a surprise to many that of all the confessional attempts at a Christian response to contemporary religious pluralism, the Roman Catholic effort seems the most open and ready to come up with new models."[110] However, it needs to be reiterated that the new theological and pastoral trends introduced by Vatican II, were not always fully appreciated nor their theological implications adequately worked out by all the local Churches. But, the questions connected with non-Christian religions continued to be more insistent than ever, and the Church had to engage in dialogue with them and develop a theology of religions suited to it, as is clear from the subsequent magisterium of the Popes, and the official documents of the Church on non-Christian religions, especially those of the Pontifical Council for Interreligious Dialogue, which we shall discuss in the next two chapters.

---

109 Edward P. Hahnenberg says that in an article published by Karl Rahner shortly after the Vatican II, he divided Christian history into three periods: a) the period of *Jewish Christianity*, relatively brief, in which followers of Jesus remained entirely within the context of Judaism; b) the period of *European Christianity* which began with the acceptance of gentiles into the Church in the first century, and extended up to the twentieth century; c) the period of *world-Church* opened by Vatican II in which the Church does not simply export a finished product, but one that openly engages other peoples, cultures and mentalities, manifested also in its openness to other religions. Cfr. Edward P. Hahnenberg, *A Concise Guide to the Documents of Vatican II*, p. 163.

110 Paul F. Knitter, *No Other Name?*, p. 120.

Chapter 4

Interreligious Dialogue in the Document *Dialogue and Mission*

The Catholic Church has been actively engaged in interreligious dialogue since the Second Vatican Council, especially after the promulgation of the landmark document *Nostra aetate*, which, as we have seen in the previous chapter, discusses the relation between the Church and the followers of other religions. Under the auspices of the Vatican Secretariat for Non-Christians the Catholic Church has undertaken many studies and published a lot of literature as guidelines for those engaged in interreligious dialogue. On 10 May 1984, the Secretariat brought out an important document entitled, "The Attitude of the Church toward Followers of Other Religions. Reflections and Orientations on Dialogue and Mission" [1], which

1 Cfr. Segretariato per i Non-Cristiani, "L'atteggiamento della Chiesa di fronte ai seguaci di altre religioni. Riflessioni e orientamenti su dialogo e missione", in *Enchiridion Vaticanum. Documenti Ufficiali della Santa Sede 1983-1985*, Vol. 9, Testo ufficiale e versione Italiana, Bologna, Centro Editoriale Dehoniano, 1987, pp.

is generally abbreviated as *Dialogue and Mission.* It was the fruit of a work which began in 1979. After Pope Paul VI's encyclical *Ecclesiam suam* of 1964, and the documents of the Second Vatican Council, especially *Nostra aetate* of 1965, *Dialogue and Mission* is undoubtedly a text of considerable importance for understanding the Catholic Church's view on interreligious dialogue during the early post-Conciliar period. This chapter, which contains some critical observations, is a brief analysis of the context, purpose and contents of this document from the perspective of interreligious dialogue.[2]

1. Occasion and content of the document

Dialogue and Mission was published by the Secretariat for Non-Christians on the occasion of the twentieth anniversary of the publication of *Ecclesiam suam* (6 August 1964)[3], and the founding of the Vatican Secretariat for Non-Christians (19 May 1964).[4] In 1984, gathered in plenary assembly, the Secretariat evaluated its experience of interreligious dialogue, and reflected on the Church's attitude towards the followers of other religions, and the relationship between dialogue and mission. The document also summarized the teaching of Vatican II on interreligious dialogue, and encouraged local Churches to establish adequate structures to promote dialogue in their respective contexts. The document is divided into three parts: a) Mission, b) Dialogue, and c) Dialogue and Mission, and consists of forty-four succinct articles.[5] Thus, the two major themes discussed in it are, the nature of the evangelising mission of the Church, and

---

928-943. (Henceforth referred to as *Dialogo e Missione*). See also *Acta Apostolicae Sedis,* 76 (1984), pp. 816-828.

2 It is to be noted that, the document deals with two key themes, namely 'interreligious dialogue' and 'Mission' ('evangelising mission of the Church'). Since our interest here is in interreligious dialogue, the aspect of mission will not be discussed in detail.

3 Cfr. *Dialogo e Missione*, no. 4.

4 Cfr. Ibid., no. 5.

5 The document *Dialogue and Mission* was signed by Francis A. Arinze (pro-president) and Marcello Zago (secretary). Cfr. Ibid., p. 943.

interreligious dialogue – and therefore the use of the abbreviated title *Dialogue and Mission*.

2. Nature and purpose of the document

The document is primarily pastoral in character, and is inspired by the Second Vatican Council and the subsequent magisterium of the Church.[6] It is meant – as the document itself states – as a help to Christians to encounter followers of other religions with whom they live in the city, at work, and in the family.[7] It is a kind of support material for Christian communities, especially leaders, to live according to the directives of the Council. The document was meant to discuss the relation between dialogue and mission because of the challenges and problems they pose.[8] There was a certain tension between the two, and the document attempts to give a solution to it. It says: "It [*Dialogue and Mission*] offers elements of a solution to the difficulties which can arise from the duties of evangelisation and dialogue which are found together in the mission of the Church."[9] It is meant also for non-Christians, inasmuch as through the document, they might also come to understand better how the Church views them, and how it intends to relate with them.[10]

6 Cfr. Ibid., no. 6. Regarding the post-Conciliar magisterium, mention may be made especially of the Apostolic Exhortation *Evangelii Nuntiandi* (8 December 1975) of Pope Paul VI, and the Encyclical *Redemptor Hominis* (4 March 1979) of Pope John Paul II. *Evangelii Nuntiandi* is entirely dedicated to the post-Vatican II theology of the Missions. In *Redemptor Hominis* there are some articles that deal with theology of religions and interreligious dialogue. Cfr. John Paul II, *Redemptor Hominis*, in *Acta Apostolicae Sedis*, 71 (1979), nos. 4, 6, 11.

7 Cfr. *Dialogo e Missione*, no. 6.

8 Cfr. Ibid., nos. 7, 36.

9 Ibid., no. 7. The quotations in English in this chapter are taken from the official English translation of *Dialogo e Missione* available in Pontifical Council for Interreligious Dialogue: "The Attitude of the Church toward Followers of Other Religions. Reflections and Orientations on Dialogue and Mission, in *Interreligious Dialogue. The Official Teaching of the Catholic Church from the Second Vatican Council to John Paul II (1963-2005)*, Francesco Gioia (ed.), Boston, Pauline Books and Media, 2006, 1116-1129.

10 Cfr. *Dialogo e Missione*, no. 7.

One may argue that, the intention of the document appears to be that, non-Christians may understand clearly that Christian efforts at dialogue with non-Christians are not aimed at their conversion to Christianity. There are many cases of non-Christians who interpret any initiative of Christians, including humanitarian services offered even in times of disasters and natural calamities, as means to convert them. Even today, many non-Christians do interpret interreligious dialogue as a new method invented by the Church to convert them. This is generally noticed among religious fundamentalist groups and those who are under their influence. The document is also offered to other Christian Churches and ecclesial communities because many of them have similar encounter experiences with followers of other religions, and in this sense, it was written with an ecumenical spirit.[11] Thus, the possible beneficiaries of the document are: all Christians in communion with the Church of Rome, other Christian Churches and ecclesial communities[12] and non-Christians – obviously in different degrees.

3. Meaning of dialogue

The document gives a short but broad definition of dialogue, and envisages it as all positive and constructive ways of relating to communities and individuals of other religions in order to promote mutual understanding and enrichment. It says: "It [dialogue] means not only discussion, but also includes all positive and constructive interreligious relations with individuals and communities of other faiths which are directed at mutual understanding and enrichment".[13] Dialogue is also described as walking together with people of other religions in order to seek truth and to work together in projects of

---

11 Cfr. Ibid., no. 8.

12 The document mentions by name the World Council of Churches. Cfr. Ibid.

13 Ibid., no. 3. The official text in Italian reads: "*Indica non solo il colloquio, ma anche l'insieme dei rapporti interreligiosi, positive e costruttivi, con una persona e comunità di altre fedi per una mutua conoscenza e un reciproco arricchimento.*"

common concern.[14] These descriptions of dialogue are important developments from Vatican II, which did not define dialogue. Again, the description of dialogue in the document is less complicated and more direct than the one given by Pope Paul VI in his *Ecclesiam suam*.

4. Reasons for dialogue

The document presents some basic reasons for Christian engagement in dialogue. We may classify them as anthropological and social, Trinitarian, Christological, Pneumatological and ecclesiological. The document itself does not use all these terms, but what they signify can be traced in it. In this sense, the document is not only pastoral but also theological.

First, the desire to dialogue is an outcome of certain personal and social requirements.[15] The need to communicate with others is something fundamental to every human being. Through interpersonal dialogue, one experiences one's own limitations and becomes aware that one does not possess the whole truth but needs to walk together with others towards that goal. Dialogue is an occasion for mutual affirmation, reciprocal correction and purification, fraternal exchange, interpersonal communion, and mutual enrichment. Christians engage in dialogue with the followers of other faiths also to listen and understand what they have to communicate, and to profit from the gifts which God has bestowed so generously in different cultures and religions. Dialogical style of human relations is demanded also by the growing interdependence in social life, for harmonious living together, human promotion, and peace.[16]

Second, the Church promotes dialogue because of her faith in God the Father. The Trinitarian mystery of Christian revelation presents Christians with a glimpse into God's life which is one of

14 Cfr. Ibid., no. 13. The text in Italian reads: "*Vi è il dialogo nel quale i cristiani incontrano i seguaci di altre tradizioni religiose per camminare insieme verso la verità e collaborare in opere di interesse comune*".

15 Cfr. Ibid., no. 21.

16 Cfr. Ibid.

communion and interchange.[17] The document says that, in the life of each individual and all peoples there is present the power of God's grace which elevates and redeems them. The Church has the duty of discovering and bringing to light and fullness, all the richness and gifts which the Father has hidden in creation and history, and to promote them among all peoples.[18] Interreligious dialogue is one of the ways of accomplishing this important task.

Third, Christians believe that Jesus Christ is God's Word and Wisdom, who enlightens every person. All human beings are redeemed by Christ, and he is united to them even when they are unaware of it. He is present with his grace in every human encounter in order to liberate human beings from their selfishness and to make them love one another.[19] This is another reason for engaging in interreligious dialogue.

Fourth, the Holy Spirit is operative in the depth of people's consciousness, and he secretly leads them towards the truth (*GS* 22). He is also present and at work outside the visible confines of the Mystical Body of Christ, which is the Church (*RH* 6; *LG* 16; *GS* 22; *AG* 15). Guided by the Spirit, the Church feels impelled to discern the signs of the times, and follow him wherever he leads her, and humbly serve and collaborate with him.[20] One of the manifestations of the action of the Spirit is inspiring people to engage in dialogue in order to seek the truth.

Fifth, the reign of God is the final end of all persons. The Church, which is to be 'its seed and beginning' (*LG* 5,9), is called from the first to start out on this path toward the realisation of the Kingdom, and, along with the rest of humanity, to advance toward that goal, which includes also the duty to struggle against evil and sin, beginning always with one's own person. Therefore, the Church is equipped and commissioned to work towards God's reign so that

17 Cfr. Ibid., no. 22.

18 Cfr. Ibid., no. 23.

19 Cfr. Ibid.

20 Cfr. Ibid., no. 24.

there comes about the progressive fulfilment of all things in Christ.[21] One of the ways in which the Church fulfils this mission entrusted to her is through dialogue.

Sixth, many positive values are found preserved in the great religious traditions of humanity. As already we have seen, Vatican II affirmed that in other religions there are 'elements which are true and good' (*OT* 16), 'precious things, both religious and human' (*GS* 92), 'seeds of contemplation' (*AG* 18), 'elements of truth and grace' (*AG* 9), 'seeds of the Word' (*AG* 11,15), and 'rays of the truth which illumine all mankind' (*NA* 2). Therefore, they merit the attention and esteem of Christians, and their spiritual patrimony is a genuine invitation to dialogue (*NA* 2,3; *AG* 11), not only in those things which unite them with Christians, but also in their differences.[22]

5. Forms of dialogue

Though there are multiple ways of dialogue, *Dialogue and Missions* presents four forms of dialogue, which it considers as the most important and typical. They are: dialogue of life, dialogue of works, dialogue of experts, and dialogue of religious experience.[23] This distinction made by the document is a major contribution to understanding the nature of interreligious dialogue. Michael L. Fitzgerald[24], maintains that, *Dialogue and Mission* was perhaps the first to present four forms of dialogue.[25]

---

21 Cfr. Ibid., no. 25.

22 Cfr. Ibid., no. 26.

23 Cfr. Ibid., nos. 29, 31, 33, 35.

24 Michael L. Fitzgerald (1937-) a native of the United Kingdom, was Secretary of the Secretariat for Non-Christians from 1987 to 2002, and President of the Pontifical Council for Interreligious Dialogue from 2002 to 2006. He was made bishop in 1992 and Archbishop in 2002. He is one of the leading experts on Islam, Muslim-Christian relations and Interreligious Dialogue.

25 Cfr. Michael L. Fitzgerald and John Borelli, *Interfaith Dialogue*, p. 28. As it will be shown later, the document *Dialogue and Proclamation* published in 1991, by the Vatican Pontifical Council for Interreligious Dialogue, will retain all these four forms of dialogue with some minor terminological changes: 'dialogue of works' (*opere*) will be translated into English as 'dialogue of action' (*opere*); 'dialogue of

5.1 Dialogue of life

The first form of dialogue is dialogue of life. *Dialogue and Mission* describes it as a manner of acting, an attitude and a spirit which guides one's behaviour. It implies concern, respect and hospitality toward the other. It leaves room for the other person's identity, modes of expression and values.[26] The document also calls this form of

---

experts' will be reworded as 'dialogue of theological exchange'; the other two forms will remain as they are. Cfr. Pontificio Consiglio per il Dialogo Interreligioso e Congregazione per l'Evangelizzazione dei Popoli, "Dialogo e annuncio: Riflessioni e orientamenti sull'annuncio del vangelo e il dialogo interreligioso", in *Enchiridion Vaticanum. Documenti Ufficiali della Santa Sede 1991-1993*, Vol. 13, Testo ufficiale e versione Italiana, Bologna, Centro Editoriale Dehoniano, 1995, no. 42. (Henceforth referred to as *Dialogo e Annuncio*). See also *Acta Apostolicae Sedis*, 84 (1992), pp. 414-446.

Obviously, there are different ways of categorising the forms of dialogue. For example, Erick Sharpe speaks of: discursive dialogue, human dialogue, secular dialogue and spiritual dialogue. Cfr. Erich J. Sharpe, "Dialogue of Religions", in Mircea Eliade (ed.), *Encyclopedia of Religion*, Vol. 4, New York, Macmillian Company, 1987, p. 347; Volker Kuester, speaks of three forms of dialogue: dialogue of life, dialogue of thought, and dialogue of heart. Cfr. Volker Küster, "Who, With Whom, About What? Exploring the Landscape of Interreligious Dialogue", in *Exchange: Journal of Missiological and Ecumenical Research*, 33:1, Brill Academic Publishers, Leiden 2004, pp. 78-79; Jane Idleman Smith speaks of such diverse models of dialogue as: dialogue of persuasion model (debate model which is already out of date), 'get to know you' model, dialogue in the classroom model, theological exchange model, ethical exchange model, dialogue about ritual model, dialogue about spirituality model, co-operative model addressing pragmatic concerns. Cfr. Jane Idleman Smith, *Muslims, Christians, and the Challenge of Interfaith Dialogue*, Oxford, Oxford University Press, 2007, 63-82; Scaria Thuruthiyil speaking of dialogue in the Indian context broadly divides dialogue into 'interior dialogue' and 'exterior dialogue'. Interior dialogue is dialogue within the Church and it is divided into Indianisation of liturgy, discernment of elements that are positive and negative in Indian and Western cultures, and inculturation of the style of life; exterior dialogue, which is dialogue of the Indian Church with Hinduism, is divided into dialogue of life, dialogue of action, dialogue of study and reflection, dialogue of prayer and religious experience, associations of dialogue, intra-personal dialogue and dialogue of reconciliation. Cfr. Scaria Thuruthiyil, *Principi e valori educativi nella tradizione Indiana*, Roma, Edizioni Progetto Cultura, 2010, 258-268.

26 Cfr. *Dialogo e Missione*, no. 29.

dialogue as 'dialogue of daily life' because every follower of Christ, by reason of his human and Christian vocation, is called to live dialogue in his daily life, whether one finds oneself in a majority situation or that of a minority. One ought to bring the spirit of the Gospel into any environment in which one lives and works, be it familial or social or educational or artistic or economic or political. Dialogue, thus, finds its place in the dynamism of the Church's mission.[27]

Edward Idris Cassidy[28] avers that dialogue of life is a true Christian witness of charity, mercy, pardon, reconciliation and peace. Thus, interreligious dialogue begins with a dialogue of life that is directed towards a friendly co-existence that enriches the partners by living out the human and spiritual values of the respective religions.[29]

Fitzgerald says that dialogue of life is not something passive or mere co-existence. It requires openness, a desire to enter into relations with others. Its aim is to establish good neighbourly relations to ensure that people live in peace and harmony.[30] This form of dialogue in the neighbourhood, at school, in the work place, concerns everybody and is within the capacity of all. It does not require any special training, but calls on qualities of the heart, such as, sympathy, respect, patience, and it is in this form of dialogue that laypeople have a particular responsibility and a special role to play.[31] Dialogue of life may appear to be spontaneous, but it does require an effort. It is easy to close in on oneself and ignore the other, especially if that other belongs to a rather closed community, which apparently does not want to enter into dialogue. It requires perseverance to

27 Cfr. Ibid., no. 30. The document *Dialogue and Proclamation*, referring to dialogue of life states that, it exists where people strive to live in an open and neighbourly spirit, sharing their joys and sorrows, their human problems and preoccupations. Cfr. *Dialogo e Annuncio*, no. 42.

28 Edward Idris Cassidy (1924-) a native of Australia, was President of the Pontifical Council for Promoting Christian Unity from 1989 to 2001, and headed the Vatican Commission for Religious Relations with the Jews. He was made a bishop on 1970 and cardinal in 1991.

29 Cfr. Edward Idris Cassidy, *Ecumenism and Interreligious Dialogue*, p. 137.

30 Cfr. Michael L. Fitzgerald and John Borelli, *Interfaith Dialogue*, p. 29.

31 Cfr. Ibid., p. 74.

overcome the barriers of diffidence and suspicion. Hence, this form of dialogue cannot be taken for granted. It has to be worked at all the time. Otherwise, outside influences can come into play and break up the existing harmony.[32]

Fitzgerald adds that, dialogue of life has a special value of its own. If one is familiar with the parable of the Good Samaritan (Jn 4: 1-30), one will certainly rate this form of dialogue very highly and place it well up on the dialogue scale.[33]

5.2 Dialogue of works

The second form of dialogue is dialogue of works. It is a dialogue of deeds and collaboration with others for goals of a humanitarian, social, economic, or political nature, which are directed towards human liberation and advancement. For example, it can be for the defence and promotion of social justice, moral values, peace and liberty. This kind of dialogue often occurs today in the context of international organisations where Christians and followers of other religions work together in order to find solutions to the problems of the world.[34] The field of collaboration can be extremely wide, and the great problems, with which humanity is struggling, call on Christians to work together with followers of other religions.[35]

Fitzgerald states that, the underlying reason for dialogue of works, which he calls 'shared action', is that good neighbourliness also means giving and receiving, and rendering mutual service. Here again there is a vast field for involvement of lay people. This form of dialogue also has a profound theological value. To work for the integral development of human beings, to strive to liberate people

32 Cfr. Ibid., p. 75. For some typical examples of 'dialogue of life' where different religions are involved, see Ibid., pp. 29-30.

33 Cfr. Ibid., p. 75.

34 Cfr. *Dialogo e Missione*, nos. 31-32. *Dialogue and Proclamation* calls this form of dialogue 'dialogue of action' and describes it as a form of dialogue in which Christians and others collaborate for the integral development and liberation of people. Cfr. *Dialogo e Annuncio*, no. 42.

35 Cfr. *Dialogo e Missione*, no. 32.

from unjust structures of oppression or poverty, is to share in the building up of the Kingdom of God. Lay people who engage in this form of dialogue are truly instruments of God's love, helping to fulfil the prayer of Jesus, 'your kingdom come'.[36] Besides, work for justice and peace is an integral part of the Church's mission, and has to be carried out at all levels. A great deal of confidence is needed to be able to work harmoniously together, and this kind of action can truly be considered a form of dialogue.[37]

5.3 Dialogue of experts

The third form of dialogue is dialogue of experts, which is of particular interest to specialists of various religions.[38] Here the Christian, without ignoring the differences that exist among religious traditions, recognises the treasures of other religions and enters into theological discussion and exchange. They study, confront, deepen, and enrich their respective religious heritages or apply something of their expertise to the problems which must be faced by humanity in the course of its history. Such a dialogue normally occurs where one's partner already has his or her own vision of the world, and adheres to a religion which inspires him or her to action. This is more easily accomplished in pluralistic societies where diverse religious traditions and ideologies coexist and sometimes come in contact.[39] In this type of dialogue, the partners come to a mutual understanding and appreciation of each other's spiritual values and cultural categories, and promote communion and fellowship among people (*NA* 1).

36 Cfr. Michael L. Fitzgerald and John Borelli, *Interfaith Dialogue*, p. 75.

37 Cfr. Ibid., pp. 31-32.

38 Cfr. *Dialogo e Missione*, no. 33. *Dialogue and Proclamation* rewords this form of dialogue as 'dialogue of theological exchange', where specialists seek to deepen their understanding of their respective religious heritages, and to appreciate each other's spiritual values. Cfr. *Dialogo e Annuncio*, no. 42. Fitzgerald says that he would have preferred 'dialogue of discourse' or 'dialogue of formal exchange' instead of 'dialogue of theological exchange', since the subject may not necessarily be confined to theological issues. Cfr. Michael L. Fitzgerald and John Borelli, *Interfaith Dialogue*, p. 28.

39 Cfr. *Dialogo e Missione*, no. 33.

Dialogue of experts is also a way in which the Christians can work together with others for the evangelical transformation of cultures (*EN* 18, 20, 63).[40]

Dialogue of experts is perhaps the most familiar type of dialogue. It can be bilateral or trilateral or multilateral with people of many different religions taking part, and each has its own special advantages. Meetings may also differ in the number of participants, ranging from large congresses to groups that can meet in people's homes. Again, the topics addressed may be theological or social issues. The way of organising the meetings can differ: the choice of participants may be through inviting individuals or institutions that select their own representatives.[41] Fitzgerald says that, in any type of formal discussion, laypeople can take an active part: reading papers, acting as discussants, or simply joining in the exchanges. Today more and more people are studying theology, and can, therefore, make an informed contribution to theological dialogue. Their presence in such formal meetings is of great significance. It helps to give a witness to what the Church really is: not just a clerical body, but the people of God.[42]

Fitzgerald says that if the dialogue of experts is to succeed, certain conditions need to be fulfilled: preparation should be carried out jointly; it should be a serious preparation that leaves room for spontaneous discussions. Care must be taken to avoid polemics, but also not to restrict the exchanges to a purely academic approach. Continuity is important because confidence grows when people meet at frequent intervals.[43]

Regarding the value of this form of dialogue, Fitzgerald states that, it is best seen, as 'walking together towards the truth'. Through honest presentations of one's views, through discussions, and above all by listening to one another, one can come to a better appreciation of the respective religious traditions of others. This form of dialogue

40 Cfr. Ibid., no. 34.

41 Cfr. Michael L. Fitzgerald and John Borelli, *Interfaith Dialogue*, p. 32.

42 Cfr. Ibid., p. 76.

43 Cfr. Ibid., pp. 32-33.

can help to remove prejudices, create understanding, and thus encourage both the dialogue of life and the dialogue of works.[44]

5.4 Dialogue of religious experience

The fourth form of dialogue is dialogue of religious experience.[45] At a deeper level, persons rooted in their own religious traditions can share their spiritual riches flowing from their experiences of prayer, contemplation, faith and duty, as well as their expressions and ways of searching for God or the Absolute. This type of dialogue can be a mutual enrichment and fruitful co-operation for promoting and preserving the highest values and spiritual ideals. It leads naturally to each partner communicating to the other the reasons for one's own faith. Sometimes profound differences can exist between religions, but it does not prevent this form of dialogue. Dialogue of religious experience also gives the Christian the opportunity to offer to the other the possibility of experimenting with the values of the Gospel in an existential way.[46]

Sharing of spiritual experiences can be done formally or spontaneously in private conversation. Joint study of religious texts, joint prayer meetings, or simply the presence of one at another's worship may mark this form of dialogue. All this requires great care, a sense of profound respect for other religions, and avoidance of any semblance of syncretism.[47] Fitzgerald says that, in dialogue of religious experience too, laypeople have a particularly valuable contribution to make. Spirituality is not restricted to priests, monks and nuns and members of religious congregations. More and more

44 Cfr. Ibid., p. 76.

45 Cfr. *Dialogo e Missione*, no. 35. *Dialogue and Proclamation* describes dialogue of religious experience as a form of dialogue where persons rooted in their own religious traditions, share their spiritual riches, for instance with regard to prayer and contemplation, faith and ways of searching for God or the Absolute. Cfr. *Dialogo e Annuncio*, no. 42.

46 Cfr. *Dialogo e Missione*, no. 35.

47 Cfr. Michael L. Fitzgerald and John Borelli, *Interfaith Dialogue*, pp. 76-77.

laypeople are studying spirituality, engaging in retreat preaching, and offering their services for spiritual direction. Such people, firmly rooted in their own religious faith, are well suited to this particular from of dialogue.[48]

6. Theological developments in *Dialogue and Mission*

Though it is true that *Dialogue and Mission* is a continuation of Vatican II, in it one comes across certain theological developments. In some cases it elaborates and clarifies what has already been said by the Council and the subsequent magisterium, but in certain other cases it goes beyond them. Though the document states that it is pastoral in character, it has also a theology of dialogue. These new developments merit an articulation that follows:

6.1 Dialogue as an integral element of Church's evangelising mission

Dialogue and Mission affirms that, interreligious dialogue is situated within the single but complex and articulated reality of the mission of the Church.[49] This means that dialogue with the followers of other religious traditions is part of the very mission of the Church. The document explains that, though the Church's mission is one, it comes to be exercised in different ways, according to the conditions in which the mission unfolds.[50] Without being exhaustive, the text identifies five fundamental elements of the *single* mission of the Church. They are: a) simple presence and *living witness* of the Christian life; b) concrete commitment to the *service of humankind* and all forms of activity for social development and for the struggle against poverty and the structures which produce it; c) *liturgical life* and that of prayer and contemplation; d) *dialogue* in which Christians meet the followers of other religious in order to walk together toward truth and to work together in projects of common

48 Cfr. Ibid., p. 77.

49 Cfr. *Dialogo e Missione*, no. 13.

50 Cfr. Ibid., no. 11.

concern; and, e) *proclamation and catechesis* in which the good news of the Gospel is preached and its consequences for life and culture are analysed. The totality of Christian mission embraces all these elements.[51] Thus, interreligious dialogue is understood as one of the elements of evangelisation, so that one can now speak of dialogue itself as a form of evangelisation. But dialogue is not a substitute for Church's mission. This is a major development in the understanding of the concept of interreligious dialogue, and it has a validity of its own. The document also states that, the life of Jesus contains all the elements of mission, including dialogue, and Christians ought to act in the same way.[52]

Jacques Dupuis says that, the direct aim of *Dialogue and Mission* was to show the place which interreligious dialogue occupies in the overall evangelising mission of the Church, thereby stating explicitly what other documents so far had left unsaid.[53] According to Cassidy, *Dialogue and Mission* is certainly a positive development in the Church's understanding of her relationship with other religions. While being firmly rooted in the Council declaration *Nostra aetate*, the document strengthens the Church's commitment to interreligious dialogue by pointing out the relationship between dialogue and mission, and then by affirming dialogue as an essential element of the Church's mission.[54] Thus, interreligious dialogue itself is a specific task of evangelisation, which finds its place in the great dynamism of the Church's mission.[55]

Pope Paul VI, while encouraging interreligious dialogue in his encyclical *Ecclesiam suam*, did not take a position on the exact place that such dialogue might occupy in the Church's mission. Similarly,

---

51 Cfr. Ibid., no. 13.

52 Cfr. Ibid., no. 15.

53 Cfr. Jacques Dupuis, "A Theologian Commentary: Dialogue and Proclamation", in William R. Burrows (ed.), *Redemption and Dialogue. Reading Redemptoris Missio and Dialogue and Proclamation*, Eugene, Wipf and Stock Publishers, 1993, p. 129.

54 Cfr. Edward Idris Cassidy, *Ecumenism and Interreligious Dialogue*, p. 149.

55 Cfr. *Dialogo e Missione*, no. 30.

Vatican II encouraged dialogue with other religions, but it did not declare it to be part of the Church's evangelising mission. This has come, for the first time, with *Dialogue and Mission*, and will be followed by other important ecclesial documents of the future.[56]

Dupuis says that Vatican II was the first Council in the conciliar history of the Church to speak positively of other religions. It made a strong appeal in favour of dialogue with the members of other religious traditions, but nowhere has the Council affirmed that interreligious dialogue is an integral part of the Church's evangelising mission. In the Conciliar documents, evangelisation remains identified with the proclamation of Jesus Christ to those who do not know him and the invitation which the Church extends to them of becoming his disciples in the Christian community (*LG* 17; *AG* 6). Whatever importance or merit may be attributed to dialogue, in terms of its relation to evangelisation, it represents but a first approach to other religions, to which the pre-Conciliar theological term of 'pre-evangelisation' could still be applied. A broader concept of the Church's evangelising mission, comprising, besides the proclamation of the Gospel, other elements such as human promotion and liberation and interreligious dialogue, is a post-Conciliar development.[57]

Dupuis further states that *Dialogue and Mission* also has a broader concept of evangelisation than that which is found in previous official documents of the Church, especially *Ad gentes* of Vatican II and *Evangelii Nuntiandi* of Pope Paul VI. In *Dialogue and Mission* there is a development from Pope Paul VI's view, because he did not assign to interreligious dialogue a place in the Church's evangelising mission as constituting an integral part of that mission. Further, his evaluation of other religions was not very positive.[58] In *Evangelii Nintiandi* his negative stand on other religions was more

56 Cfr. http://tomryancsp.org/proclamation.htm (22.1.2014).

57 Cfr. Jacques Dupuis, *Toward a Christian Theology of Religious Pluralism,* p. 359; Id., "A Theologian Commentary: Dialogue and Proclamation", p. 124.

58 In chapter two we have already seen this famous statement: "Indeed, honesty compels us to declare openly our conviction that the Christian religion is the one and only true religion." Paul VI, *Ecclesiam suam,* no. 107, p. 655.

striking, and he saw them as 'natural religions'[59] and Christianity as the supernatural religion. It must be further noted that, *Evangelii Nuntindi* no longer speaks of dialogue with the members of other religions, though the concept of evangelisation proposed is broad even as to include human liberation.[60] Hence, considering dialogue as an integral element of evangelisation marks a *significant qualitative change* in post-Conciliar mission theology. It forms part of the development in post-Vatican II years of a broad and comprehensive notion of evangelisation, of which dialogue, together with other elements, is an integral dimension. The breakthrough came with documents belonging to the 1980s and 1990s[61], and *Dialogue and Mission* may be considered as the first official witness to it.

6.2 Dialogue as witness to Christian faith

One of the principal ways of carrying out the evangelising mission of the Church is through witness of Christian life. In interreligious dialogue, the most evident element of evangelisation is witness of life, because in genuine dialogue, the Christian shares his experience of Christ with his brothers and sisters of another religion.[62] Therefore, Christians are asked to engage in sincere and patient dialogue with people of other faiths with whom they live. They ought to know well the religious and cultural traditions of others, to be happy to discover and ready to respect the 'seeds of the Word' which are hidden in them, and to learn by sincere and patient dialogue, what treasures a bountiful God has distributed among the nations of the earth. At the same time, they ought to illumine these treasures with the light of the Gospel, to set them free, and bring them under

59 Cfr. Paul VI, *Evangelii Nuntiandi*, in *Acta Apostolicae Sedis,* 68 (1976), no. 53.

60 Cfr. Jacques Dupuis, "A Theologian Commentary: Dialogue and Proclamation", p. 126.

61 Cfr. Jacques Dupuis, *Toward a Christian Theology of Religious Pluralism,* p. 359.

62 Cfr. *Dialogo e Missione*, no. 40.

the dominion of God and Saviour (*AG* 11; *AG* 41; *AA* 14,29).[63] In this way, dialogue provides a Christian the opportunity to share with others, in an existential way, the values of the Gospel.[64] Hence, dialogue necessarily implies the witness of Christian life, without which no credible evangelising activity can be spoken of. Dupuis says: "This conclusion confirms once more that dialogue – informed by witness, as it must be in all circumstances – is by itself a form of evangelisation, even in the absence of proclamation."[65]

6.3 New understanding of conversion

Dialogue and Mission says that, in the context of dialogue between believers of various faiths, one cannot avoid reflecting on the spiritual process of conversion.[66] Then it proceeds to give two distinct interpretations of the term 'conversion'. The first meaning of the term is based on biblical language and Christian tradition. Here, conversion is understood as the humble and penitent return of the heart to God in the desire to submit one's life more generously to him. In this sense, all persons are constantly called to conversion.[67] In the second sense, conversion means the free decision to change one's religious adherence. The document says that, in the course of the process dialogue, the decision may be made by someone to leave one's previous spiritual or religious situation in order to direct oneself toward another.[68] It also adds that, in process of conversion, the law of conscience is sovereign[69], that the principal agent of conversion is not human beings but the Holy Spirit, and that the Christian is but a simple instrument and co-worker of God.[70] This interpretation of

63 Cfr. Ibid., no. 27.

64 Cfr. Ibid., no. 35.

65 Jacques Dupuis, "A Theological Commentary: *Dialogue and Proclamation*", p. 148.

66 Cfr. *Dialogo e Missione*, no. 37.

67 Cfr. Ibid.

68 Cfr. Ibid.

69 Cfr. Ibid., no. 38.

70 Cfr. Ibid., no. 39.

conversion can go a long way to clarify the misunderstanding often prevalent among some followers of other religions who think that the Christian initiative in interreligious dialogue is a 'new devise' invented to convert them to Christianity.[71]

According to the above interpretation, the kind of conversion aimed at in dialogue is not the conversion of the partner in dialogue to one's own religious tradition, but a common deepening of both partners' conversion to God. It is a conversion understood in the biblical sense of *metanoia* (change in one's way of life and mentality resulting from penitence or spiritual conversion) which is comprehensive enough to cover all the fundamental aspects of life, personal and social, which lead to positive changes. Conversion in this sense is open to all, to whatever religious tradition they may belong.

But, as we have seen above, the document also cautiously adds that, in the process of conversion to God, the decision may be made to leave one's previous spiritual or religious situation in order to direct oneself toward another. This can happen to any partner in dialogue, including the Christian. But the document clearly states that this form of conversion should take place in accordance with the principles of religious liberty, freedom of conscience, human rights and dignity, and that there should be no force or coercion.[72]

Therefore, dialogue does not serve as a means to the end of converting others to one's own religion, as some might be erroneously led to believe. Neither on one side nor on the other, does it tend to the conversion of one's partners to one's own religious faith. Rather, it tends toward a deeper conversion of each person to God. In this sense, the proper end of interreligious dialogue is ultimately the *common conversion* of Christians and the members of other religious traditions to the same God. This is one of the important and positive

71 Here, it is important to note that, in the Roman Catholic Church, the Vatican Congregation for the Evangelisation of Peoples, and the Pontifical Council for Interreligious Dialogue are two distinct dicasteries. This institutional separation also points to the fact that the scope of interreligious dialogue is not conversion.

72 Cfr. *Dialogo e Missione*, nos. 18-19, 37-39.

fruits of dialogue. Hence, those who think that Christians enter into dialogue as a covert way of trying to bring about conversions to Christianity are grossly mistaken[73], and such a perception has much to do with their ignorance of the position of the Catholic Church.

6.4 Dialogical spirit as norm and style in mission

Another emphasis of the document is that dialogue is not only a distinct aspect of evangelisation, but also an 'attitude and a spirit' which must permeate every aspect of the mission of the Church. It is therefore a norm, an indispensable style, the spirit, and the necessary manner in which the Church should carry out her mission, whether it be simple presence and witness or service and human development or liturgical life or direct proclamation and catechesis or any other. All these forms of mission must be 'permeated by a dialogical spirit'. The document states: "Any sense of mission not permeated by such a dialogical spirit would go against the demands of true humanity and against the teachings of the Gospel."[74] Thus, as Dupuis says, the 'spirit of dialogue' must *inform* all the expressions of the Church's evangelising mission.[75] This possibility of a 'universal applicability' of the spirit of dialogue is another novelty of the document, and a further development from *Ecclesiam suam* which spoke of four concentric circles of dialogue.[76]

6.5 Dialogue as an obligation for all Christians

The document further affirms that interreligious dialogue is not something that is left to the choice of a Christian, but an obligation for every member of the Church. The declaration makes it clear

---

73 The document says: "Dialogue does not grow out of the opportunism of the tactics of the moment". Ibid., no. 20. The text in Italian reads: *"Il dialogo non scaturisce da opportunismi tattici dell'ora"*.

74 Ibid., no. 29.

75 Cfr. Jacques Dupuis, *Toward a Christian Theology of Religious Pluralism,* p. 363.

76 Cfr. Paul VI, *Ecclesiam suam*, nos. 97, 107, 109, 113, pp. 650, 654-655, 657.

that, contrary to the widespread thinking in the Church in the years following the Vatican II, interreligious dialogue cannot be reserved to specialists. Since every Christian is called to mission, every member of the Church is expected to promote dialogue. The document says that every Christian, by virtue of his faith and baptism, is called to carry out, to some degree, the whole mission of the Church.[77] In this, they are to follow the example of Christ[78], the early Church[79] and illustrious missionaries.[80] It also adds that every local Church is responsible for the totality of mission[81], which naturally includes also interreligious dialogue, and that the text of the document is meant as guidelines, especially for Church leaders.[82] What is implied here is that local Churches are to set up suitable structures for dialogue, and actively promote it among the faithful.

6.6 Ecumenical spirit in dialogue

Another emphasis of the document is on the importance of ecumenical spirit in dialogue. It states that many Christian Churches have rich experiences of encounter with followers of other religions. Then it makes a special reference to the World Council of Churches which has a sub-unit for "Dialogue with People of Living Faiths and Ideologies", and states that the Vatican Secretariat for Non-Christians has stable and fraternal contacts of consultation and collaboration with it.[83] Thus, the insistence on ecumenical spirit in interreligious dialogue, and the specific mention of the World Council of Churches are also among the novelties of the document.

77 Cfr. *Dialogo e Missione*, no. 14.

78 Cfr. Ibid., no. 15.

79 Cfr. Ibid., no. 16.

80 Cfr. Ibid., no. 17.

81 Cfr. Ibid., no. 14.

82 Cfr. Ibid., no. 7.

83 Cfr. Ibid., no. 8.

6.7 Other aspects

Some of the other aspects of dialogue mentioned in the document are that dialogue is a means for evangelisation and transformation of cultures[84], for promotion of genuine peace;[85] a source of hope of communion and unity of the human race;[86] a way to overcome racial, social and religious differences;[87] a path to mutual enrichment and mutual transformation of individuals and communities to build a new humanity under the guidance of the Spirit[88], etc. The document also mentions that in the Church's dialogue none is excluded, but includes all those who have respect for human values, and even those who oppose the Church and persecute her in various ways.[89] In themselves these ideas are not anything new in the magisterium of the Church on dialogue, but the document presents them inasmuch as they are ideals, perennial values and lasting fruits, and methods to be used in any genuine dialogue.

7. A critical appreciation

After having analysed the nature and contents of *Dialogue and Mission* we shall now make some critical observations on the same, highlighting some of its positive and negative aspects.

The document is the result of continuous reflection on the teachings of Vatican II and post-Conciliar magisterium on non-Christian religions. As we have seen, it interprets dialogue as all positive and constructive interreligious relations with individuals and communities of other faiths that are directed towards mutual understanding and enrichment. For the first time, dialogue is also defined as walking together with people of other religions in order to seek truth and to work together in projects of common concern.

---

84 Cfr. Ibid., nos. 34, 41.

85 Cfr. Ibid., no. 42.

86 Cfr. Ibid., no. 43.

87 Cfr. Ibid., no. 44.

88 Cfr. Ibid., no. 42.

89 Cfr. Ibid.

Here, one notices a *significant development in the understanding of the concept of dialogue.*

The document affirms that dialogue is an authentic expression of the Church's evangelising mission in its own right, and possesses its own validity, and therefore, has no need for further justification. In this sense, it is *not a means to evangelisation* as it was understood by many in the early decades of the development of the concept. This affirmation means that dialogue is a necessary norm for Christians.

Another merit of the document is that it *clarifies the concept of conversion* and states that, all the partners in dialogue are subject to conversion to God, understood as *metanoia*. This is a very important statement as far as non-Christians are concerned, as they often have the fear that interreligious dialogue is a new tactic used by Christians to convert them.

The document has furnished many *practical guidelines for dialogue,* especially through the four forms of dialogue. It is a further development from *Nostra aetate* and other Conciliar documents, and it is one of the novelties of the text.

The four forms of dialogue deals with all the principal dimensions of Christian life shared with the followers of other religions. In them is implied a *pedagogy of dialogue*, as it develops gradually from dialogue of daily life, and climaxes in the deepest form of dialogue, which is dialogue of religious experience.

When the document speaks about the 'spirit of dialogue' or 'dialogical spirit', it brings out clearly the *universal applicability of dialogue*. The dialogical spirit is not something that belongs only to the Church's mission; rather it belongs to the dynamism of human life itself. This is clear from the four forms of dialogue which the document proposes. In fact, the spirit of dialogue affects every aspect of human life: personal, social, cultural, economic, political, religious, etc. It can be applied at home, in work places, in villages and cities, and beyond the boundaries of religions and ideologies. In this sense, the 'spirit of dialogue' is more than something that must inform every aspect of the evangelising mission of the Church. It has a universal applicability inasmuch as it belongs to the very structure of the human person because every person is ontologically relational.

Notwithstanding the positive attitude towards other religions, the document seems to state implicitly that not everything in other religions is good, and that there are things that need to be illuminated with the light of the Gospel: "[...] let them try to illuminate these treasures with the light of the Gospel, to set them free and bring them under the dominion of God their Saviour."[90] This need not be interpreted as implying the superiority of Christianity over other religions, but simply as an affirmation of the fact that *in every religion there are some core convictions and non-negotiables*[91], an example of which is the above statement.

The document invites all Christians to engage in dialogue, to love, respect, esteem and study other religions, and appreciate whatever is good in them. In this sense, it proposes a *spirituality of dialogue* to be practised by all, taking into consideration the cultural conditions and attention to the signs of the times.

As for the 'negative' aspects *Dialogue and Mission*, the following observations may be made:

The title of the document is 'dialogue and mission' and it points to the fact that there is no question of a Christian choosing between dialogue and mission, but one has a duty of doing both mission and dialogue. Unfortuntely in the document, the mutual relation between dialogue and mission is not properly clarified, and there seems to be a *conflict* between the two, and it can raise *theological and pastoral problems.* Cassidy has carefully analysed some of the theological and pastoral problems the document poses. He says that *Dialogue and Mission* raises the question of how dialogue is to be related to the duty of the Church to proclaim Jesus Christ to the world. Does this mean that proclamation is now obsolete, as some missionaries are saying? Has dialogue become the new name of mission? Or is dialogue simply another way of bringing about

---

90 Ibid., no. 27.

91 Jesus Christ is Son of God, the only mediator, and the only Saviour, is a non-negotiable of Christianity.

conversion to the Christian Church? These are important questions which cannot be eluded. On the one hand, there is the danger of it sapping the missionary vitality of the Church, and on the other hand there is the risk of arousing the suspicions of people of other religions with regard to the purpose of dialogue. He then adds that, taking into consideration these issues, the decision was taken by the Secretariat for Non-Christians to produce a new document that would study the relationship between dialogue and mission, which resulted in the document *Dialogue and Proclamation* of 1991.[92]

The document cannot totally free itself from the 'allegation' that dialogue is aimed at conversion, inasmuch as it says, "In the course of this [dialogue] process, the decision may be made to leave one's previous spiritual or religious situation in order to direct oneself toward another."[93] Thus, conversion is implied. Though the document gives it only secondary importance, the statement can still be *used by critics to argue that conversion is also one of the aims of dialogue.*

The document does not discuss the question of the *role of other religious traditions themselves in the salvation of their members.* It omits the Vatican II understanding of other religions as 'preparation for the Gospel' (*LG* 16; *AG* 3), and the expression 'dialogue of salvation'.[94] One wonders why in a document that discusses the general principles of dialogue and mission, *Muslims and Islam are mentioned specially*[95], leaving out other major world religions. Though the document has Christological, Trinitarian, Pneumatological, ecclesiological and scriptural elements, one *does not find any direct reference to the*

92 Cfr. Edward Idris Cassidy, *Ecumenism and Interreligious Dialogue,* p. 150.

93 *Dialogo e Missione,* no. 37. The text in Italian reads: "*In questo processo può nascere la decisione di lasciare una situazione spirituale o religiosa anteriore per dirigersi verso un'altra.*"

94 This was a very important concept in *Ecclesiam suam.* Cfr. Paul VI, *Ecclesiam suam,* nos. 70-77, pp. 641-643. Pope John Paul II also referred to it in his *Redemptor Hominis.* Cfr. John Paul II, *Redemptor Hominis,* no. 4.

95 Cfr. *Dialogo e Missione,* nos. 17, 32. In the Italian text the terms used are "*saraceni*", "*mondo islamico*" and "*musulmani*".

Fathers of the Church, except indirectly, when it refers to some of the statements found in the documents of Vatican II.[96] The document does not say anything about the *interdependence* between the various forms of dialogue. The question of *dialogue and culture* is mentioned only in passing, and yet religions are intimately linked to cultures. *Formation to dialogue* hardly gets any attention in the text. *Fruits of dialogue* are not treated in a systematic way, and *obstacles* to dialogue are hardly discussed. In this sense, *Dialogue and Mission* can be considered as a modest document, nevertheless important, because in it one sees some clear developments from the theology of Vatican II on dialogue.

8. Conclusion

Dialogue and Mission is basically a continuation of the Vatican II programme on interreligious dialogue. But in it one also notices a development in the understanding of the theology of dialogue, which is a sign of the working of the Holy Spirit who is leading the Church into the fullness of truth. The greatest emphasis of the document is undoubtedly that interreligious dialogue is an essential dimension of the Church's mission, and that it has a validity of its own. The document was produced at a time when the legitimacy of interreligious dialogue in the mission of the Church was questioned by many within the Church, and its importance was downplayed, due to ignorance, indifference, lack of formation, and neglect in implementing the magisterium of Vatican II. This was especially noticed in seminaries, parishes, dioceses, regional ecclesiastical organisations, religious congregations, Catholic educational institutions, movements and associations. At this critical juncture, the document served the purpose of creating a new awareness in the Church regarding the importance of interreligious dialogue, according to the mandate of the Vatican II and the immediate post-Conciliar magisterium. Today *Dialogue and Mission* is, by and large, a 'forgotten document', inasmuch as it is 'taken over', 'built upon',

96 Cfr. Ibid., no. 26.

and 'overshadowed' by *Dialogue and Proclamation* published by the same Secretariat in 1991. Yet, in order to understand the theology of dialogue of this new document, and the later magisterium of the Church on dialogue, a good knowledge of *Dialogue and Mission* seems indispensable.

Chapter 5

Interreligious Dialogue in the Document *Dialogue and Proclamation*

The document *Dialogue and Proclamation*[1] was published on the occasion of the twenty-fifth anniversary of the Declaration

1 The full title is: "Dialogue and Proclamation. Reflection and Orientations on Interreligious Dialogue and the Proclamation of the Gospel of Jesus Christ" Cfr. Pontifical Council for Interreligious Dialogue, *Interreligious Dialogue. The Official Teachings of the Catholic Church from the Second Vatican Council to John Paul II (1963.2005)*, Francesco Gioia (ed.), Boston, Pauline Books and Media, 2006, p. 1156. (Abbreviated as *Dialogue and Proclamation*). In this chapter, except for the direct citations in English, all references to *Dialogue and Proclamtion* are from its original Italian text: Pontificio Consiglio per il Dialogo Interreligioso e Congregazione per l'Evangelizzazione dei Popoli, "Dialogo e Annuncio: Riflessioni e orientamenti sull'annuncio del vangelo e il dialogo interreligioso", in *Enchiridion Vaticanum. Documenti Ufficiali della Santa Sede 1991-1993*, Vol. 13, Testo ufficiale e versione Italiana, Bologna, Centro Editoriale Dehoniano, 1995, 191-229. (Henceforth referred to as *Dialogo e Annuncio*).

Nostra aetate.[2] It was a joint document of the Pontifical Council for Interreligious Dialogue (previously known as the Secretariat for Non-Christians) and the Congregation for Evangelisation of Peoples, and was published on 19 May 1991.[3] It builds upon the previous document *Dialogue and Mission* (1984) which stated that, interreligious dialogue and proclamation of the Gospel are two distinct elements of the *one* evangelising mission of the Church, and wants to elaborate further on these two components of mission, and show how they are related to each other. The document is addressed to all Catholics in communion with the Church of Rome, especially all those who have a leadership role in the community and those engaged in the work of formation. It is proposed also to the Christians belonging to other Churches or Ecclesial Communities, and to the followers of other religions, who might also be interested in it.[4] This chapter is a brief presentation of the main ideas contained in the document on interreligious dialogue, and its relation to proclamation, with some critical observations.

1. Immediate context of the document

Dialogue and Mission of 1984 had recognised the legitimate place of interreligious dialogue in the single but complex mission of the Church, and both proclamation and dialogue were viewed as authentic forms of the one evangelising mission of the Church.[5] But it raised the question of how dialogue was to be related to the duty of the Church to proclaim Jesus Christ to the world. As we have already hinted at in the preceding chapter, many saw a *conflict* between interreligious dialogue and the Lord's command to proclaim the Gospel. Some began to ask whether proclamation has now become obsolete or has dialogue become the new name for the mission of the Church or dialogue is simply another way of

2 Cfr. *Dialogo e Annuncio*, no. 1.

3 Cfr. *Dialogo e Annuncio*, no. 3. The alternative date of its publication is 21 June 1991.

4 Cfr. *Dialogo e Annuncio*, no. 7.

5 Cfr. *Dialogo e Missione*, no. 13; *Dialogo e Annuncio*, no. 2.

bringing about conversion to the Christian faith. Some also realised that, on the one hand, this situation could sap the missionary vitality of the Church, and on the other hand, arouse the suspicion of the followers of other religions with regard to the purpose of dialogue. Thus there were theological and pastoral problems connected with the teachings of *Dialogue and Mission.* As said earlier, the Secretariat for Non-Christians recognised the problem, and took the decision to publish a new document that would study, explain and clarify the relationship between dialogue and proclamation, which resulted in the document *Dialogue and Proclamation* of 1991.[6] As this document was in its final stages of preparation for publication, Pope John Paul II gave the Church his encyclical *Redemptoris Missio* (7 December 1990), in which he addressed, among other questions, the relation between dialogue and proclamation of the Gospel. *Dialogue and Proclamation* spelt out in greater detail the teaching of the encyclical on dialogue and its relationship to proclamation, and insisted that it should be read in the light of the encyclical.[7]

Jacques Dupuis says that, *Dialogue and Proclamation* was the result of long period of study and wide consultation, beginning in December 1986 and ending in 1991. It saw as many as five drafts, the first two by the Secretariat for Non-Christians, the third and fourth drafts by both the Secretariat for Non-Christians and the Congregation for Evangelisation of Peoples together, and the fifth and final draft by three dicasteries, the third being the Congregation for Doctrine of Faith. The final text approved by the heads of the three dicasteries, and signed by Cardinals Francis Arinze of the Secretariat for Non-Christians, and Joseph Tomko, the Prefect of the Congregation for Evangelisation of Peoples, was later sent to the Secretariat of State for approval and publication, which took place on 19 May 1991.[8]

6 Cfr. Edward Idris Cassidy, *Ecumenism and Interreligious Dialogue,* p. 150.

7 Cfr. *Dialogo e Annuncio*, no. 4.

8 Cfr. Jacques Dupuis, "A Theological Commentary: Dialogue and Proclamation", pp. 121-123.

2. Relevance of the document

Dialogue and Proclamation discusses some of the current situations of the world as factors that make the document relevant, and they are the following: a) a new awareness of the fact of religious pluralism; b) the hesitant practice of interreligious dialogue in some places, and the need to stimulate it; c) the problems raised by the practice of dialogue in the minds of many people; d) to spell out in greater detail the teachings of the encyclical *Redemptoris Missio* on dialogue and its relationship to proclamation;[9] e) to study, in the light of World Day of Peace in Assisi on 27 October 1986, the significance of interreligious dialogue while affirming the Church's duty to announce Jesus Christ to the world, and the fundamental unity of the human race in its origin and destiny;[10] and f) the encouragement of Pope John Paul II to promote *both* dialogue and proclamation without neglecting or ignoring one or the other.[11]

3. Meaning of some key terms

Dialogue and Proclamation begins by clarifying the key concepts of evangelisation, dialogue, proclamation, conversion, and religions and religious traditions.

The term 'evangelising mission' or 'evangelisation' is used in a *broad sense* to mean the mission of the Church in its totality;[12] and when 'evangelisation' is taken *more specifically*, it means 'proclamation', to signify the clear and unambiguous preaching of the Gospel.[13]

---

9 Cfr. *Dialogo e Annuncio*, no. 4.

10 Cfr. Ibid., no. 5.

11 Cfr. Ibid., no. 6; *Insegnamenti di Giovanni Paolo II*, Vol. IX part 2, Città del Vaticano, Libreria Editrice Vaticana, 1986, pp. 1249-51; 2019-2030.

12 Cfr. *Dialogo e Annuncio*, nos. 2, 8. As we have already seen, *Dialogue and Mission* had identified five fundamental elements of the single mission of the Church. They are implied here, namely, a) living witness of the Christian life; b) commitment to the service of humankind; c) liturgical life; d) interreligious dialogue, and, e) proclamation and catechesis. Cfr. *Dialogo e Missione*, no. 13.

13 Cfr. *Dialogo e Annuncio*, no. 8.

The term 'dialogue' is used in three senses: a) as something purely anthropological and social to mean 'reciprocal communication'; b) as 'spirit of dialogue', understood as an attitude of respect and friendship, which permeates or should permeate all those activities constituting the evangelising mission of the Church; and c) as 'all positive and constructive interreligious relations' with individuals and communities of other faiths which are directed at mutual understanding and enrichment in obedience to truth and respect for freedom. *Dialogue and Proclamation* uses the term 'dialogue' mainly in the third sense.[14]

The term 'proclamation' is used in the document to mean the communication of the Gospel message, an invitation to a commitment of faith in Jesus Christ, entry into the Church through baptism, and catechesis. It envisages proclamation as the foundation, centre, and summit of evangelisation.[15]

Dialogue and Proclamation uses term 'conversion' in two senses: a) a general movement towards God which implies a humble and penitent return of the heart to God (*metanoia*) in the desire to submit one's life more generously to him; and b) a change of religious adherence.[16]

The terms 'religion or religious traditions' are used in a generic and analogical sense to cover the religions which refer back to the faith of Abraham, as well as the religious traditions of Asia, Africa and elsewhere.[17] The document does not envisage dialogue with 'New Religious Movements'.[18]

14 Cfr. Ibid., no. 9. The second and third meaning of dialogue are clearly borrowed from *Dialogue and Mission*, nos. 3, 29.

15 Cfr. *Dialogo e Annuncio*, no. 10.

16 Cfr. Ibid., no. 11. The meaning of conversion here is taken from *Dialogue and Mission* no. 37.

17 Cfr. *Dialogo e Annuncio*, no. 12.

18 Cfr. Ibid., no. 13.

4. Theology of religions of the document

Dialogue and Proclamation has a positive theology of religions. It says that, for a just appraisal of non-Christian religions, besides theoretical knowledge, one needs to have close contact with them, practical experience of dialogue with them, and a correct theological evaluation of them. One should also approach them with great sensitivity because of the spiritual and human values enshrined in them. They should be taken seriously because over the centuries, they have borne witness to the efforts to find answers to the profound mysteries of the human condition (*NA* 1), and have given expression to religious experience, and they continue to do so today.[19]

4.1 Influence of the theology of Vatican II

The theology of *Dialogue and Proclamation* is deeply influenced by Vatican II. It reaffirms the traditional doctrine according to which salvation in Jesus Christ is, in a mysterious way, a reality open to all people of good will in whose hearts grace is active invisibly (*GS* 22).[20] He is at work in each human person to bring about interior renewal.[21] The text then uses several expressions taken from the documents of Vatican II to refer to the presence of God in non-Christian religions, such as, 'a ray of that Truth which enlightens all' (*NA* 2), 'seeds of the word' and 'riches which a generous God has distributed among the nations' (*AG* 11), the good which is 'found sown' not only 'in minds and hearts' but also 'in the rites and customs of peoples' (*LG* 17)[22], 'the universal action of the Spirit in the world before Christ was glorified' (*AG* 4), 'a preparation for the Gospel' (*LG* 16), and therefore, the need to enter into 'dialogue and collaboration' (*NA* 2; *GS* 92-93), and the obligation to acknowledge, preserve and encourage the spiritual and moral good found among them, as

---

19 Cfr. Ibid., no. 14.

20 Cfr. *Gaudium et Spes*, no. 22; *Dialogo e Annuncio*, no. 15.

21 Cfr. Ibid.

22 Cfr. Ibid., no. 16.

well as their social and cultural values (*NA* 2).[23] The document also affirms the necessity of Church's missionary activity in order to perfect in Christ these elements already found in other religions, and to preserve, heal, ennoble and perfect whatever good is found to be sown in the hearts and minds of people, or in the rites and cultures of peoples (*AG* 9).[24]

4.2 Scriptural foundations

The theology of religions of *Dialogue and Proclamation* is solidly founded on the Scriptures. By referring to the Old Testament it affirms that, God's activity extends beyond the confines of the chosen people, Israel. In order to substantiate this claim, it mentions the covenant which God made with all peoples at the beginning of creation (Gen 1-11), the covenant with Noah (Gen 9:8-17), the non-Israelite figures in the New Testament like Abel, Enoch and Noah who are proposed as models of faith (Heb 11:4-7), the prophets who brought a universal perspective of salvation that extends beyond and through Israel to the nations (Is 52:10), the Wisdom literature where the action of God is presented as to going beyond the boundaries of the chosen people in order to touch both the history of nations and the lives of individuals. The document then presents the history of salvation as having its final fulfilment in Jesus Christ who established the new and definitive covenant for all peoples.[25]

Referring to the New Testament, the document emphasises the universal character of the mission of Jesus, which went beyond the lost sheep of Israel, and manifested an open attitude towards all peoples. He entered into dialogue with gentiles and recognised the good that was in them.[26] His invitation to enter into the Kingdom of God was not confined only to the chosen people but also to all peoples.

23 Cfr. Ibid., no. 17.

24 Cfr. Ibid., no. 18.

25 Cfr. Ibid., no. 19.

26 The centurion (Mt 8:5-13), the healing miracles for 'foreigners' (Mk 7: 24-30; Mt 15: 21-28), the Samaritan woman (Jn 4:1-23) are some examples of it. Cfr. *Dialogo e Annuncio*, no. 21.

In fact, he explicitly announced the entry of the gentiles into the Kingdom of God[27], which was both historical and eschatological.[28] Non Israelites have access to the Kingdom of God in history through obedience in faith and conversion to the God of the Kingdom.[29] The preaching of the Apostles was a call directed to all peoples, and the *Acts of the Apostles* testifies to Paul's positive and open attitude towards the gentiles.[30] Again, in the New Testament, Jesus is the Word of God that enlightens everyman (Jn 1:9) and the desire of the nations.[31]

4.3 Fathers of the first centuries of the Church

Dialogue and Proclamation refers to the writings of four Fathers of the Church of the first centuries of Christianity where one finds an early tradition which was remarkably open towards people of other religions. It mentions Justin Martyr (c. 100-165) who spoke of the 'seeds' sown by the Logos in the religious traditions, and the complete manifestation of the Logos in the incarnation of Christ;[32] to Irenaeus of Lyon (c.120-c.202) who taught that the Son, the visible manifestation of the Father, had revealed himself to mankind 'from the beginning', but the incarnation brought about something entirely

27 For example, Mt 8:10-11; Mt 11:20-24; Mt 25:31-32,34; Cfr. *Dialogo e Annuncio*, no. 22.

28 Cfr. Ibid.

29 Cfr. Jacques Dupuis, *Toward a Christian Theology of Religious Pluralism*, p. 344. *Redemptoris Missio* says that the Kingdom is present in the whole of humankind to the extent that they live Gospel values and are open to the Spirit. Cfr. John Paul II, *Redemptoris Missio*, no. 20.

30 Cfr. Acts 14:8-18; 17: 22-34; Cfr. *Dialogo e Annuncio*, no. 23.

31 Cfr. Ibid.

32 Cfr. Justin Martyr, *The First Apology*, in *The Fathers of the Church. A New Translation*, Vol. 6, Hermigild Dressler (ed.), *Writings of Saint Justin Martyr*, Thomas B. Falls (tr.), Washington, The Catholic University Press of America, [1948], 2008, 46, pp. 83-84; *The Second Apology*, in *The Fathers of the Church. A New Translation*, Vol. 6, Hermigild Dressler (ed.), *Writings of Saint Justin Martyr*, Thomas B. Falls (tr.), Washington, The Catholic University Press of America, [1948], 2008, 8, pp. 127-128; 10, pp. 129-130; 13, p. 133-134.

new;[33] to Clement of Alexandria (c.150-c.215) who stated that 'philosophy' was given to the Greeks by God as a 'covenant', and as a 'stepping stone to the philosophy which was according to Christ'.[34] For these Fathers, prior to and outside the Christian dispensation, God had already, in an incomplete way, manifested himself, and the full manifestation of the Logos was in Jesus Christ.[35] The document also refers to a theology of history which becomes salvation history, because God progressively manifests himself and communicates with humankind through it. It refers to Irenaeus who spoke of the four 'covenants' given by God to the human race: in Adam, in Noah, in Moses and in Jesus Christ.[36] There is also a reference to a fourth Father of the Church, Augustine (354-430), who in his later works, stressed the universal presence and influence of the mystery of Christ even before the incarnation so that, in a certain sense, Christianity already existed 'at the beginning of the human race'.[37] He wrote: "In fact, what is now called the Christian religion existed already among the ancients, and was not absent even at the origin of the human race, until Christ came in the flesh. It was then that the true religion, which already existed, began to be called Christian [....] That is why I said: *This is in our time the Christian religion*, not because at one time it did not exist, but because it later took this name."[38]

---

33 Cfr. Irenaeus of Lyons, *Aganist Heresies*, The Complete English Translation from the first volume of *The Ante-Nicene Fathers,* Alexander Roberts, James Donaldson, A. Cleveland Coxe (eds.), Marston Gate, Ex Fontibus, new edition, 2010, 4,6.5-7; 4,7.2; 4,20.6-7, pp. 409-412, 460-462.

34 Cfr. Clement of Alexandria, *Miscellanies (Stromata),* Memphis, Bottom of the Hill Publishing, 2012, 1,5; 6,8, pp. 19, 278.

35 Cfr. *Dialogo e Annuncio*, no. 24.

36 Cfr. Irenaeus of Lyons, *Aganist Heresies*, 3,11.8, p. 312.

37 Cfr. *Dialogo e Annuncio*, no. 25.

38 Augustine, *Le Ritrattazioni,* Testo Latino dell'edizione maurina confrontato con il corpus Christianorum, Ubaldo Pizzani (tr.), Roma, Citta Nuova Editrice, 1994, 1,13.3, p. 71. (Translation is mine).

4.4 Magisterium of the Church after Vatican II

After the Vatican II, the magisterium of Pope John Paul II played a major role in the development of the theology of religions, especially through his teaching on the operative presence of the Holy Spirit in the life of the members of other religions[39], the universal action of the Holy Spirit in the world before the Christian dispensation, the universal action of the same Spirit today, even outside the visible body of the Church[40], and the mysterious presence of the Spirit in the heart of every person, Christian or otherwise.[41] He also spoke of the mystery of the unity of all humankind due to the *common origin* of all men and women, the call to a *common destiny* in the fullness of life in God, and the *unity of salvation* for all humankind in Jesus Christ.[42] From all this, the pope concluded to a 'mystery of unity' in spite of the difference between religious professions.[43] Christians know it through their faith while others remain unaware of the source of their salvation. The mystery of salvation reaches out to them, in a way known to God, through the invisible action of the Spirit of Christ. Concretely, it will be in the sincere practice of what is good in their own religious traditions, and by following the dictates of their conscience, that the members of other religions respond positively to God's invitation and receive salvation in Jesus Christ, even while they do not recognise or acknowledge him as their saviour (*AG* 3,9,11).[44] These elements, when taken together, constitute a theological basis for a positive approach to other religions and a foundation for the practice of interreligious dialogue.[45]

39 Cfr. John Paul II, *Redemptor Hominis*, in *Insegnamenti di Giovanni Paolo II*, Vol. II, part 1, Città del Vaticano, Libreria Editrice Vaticana, 1979, no. 6.

40 Cfr. John Paul II, *Dominem et Vivificatem*, in *Acta Apostolicae Sedis*, 78 (1986), no. 53.

41 Cfr. *Insegnamenti di Giovanni Paolo II*, Vol. IX, part 2, pp. 1227-1228.

42 Cfr. John Paul II, *Redemptor Hominis*, no. 13.

43 Cfr. John Paul II, *Insegnamenti* 1986, Vol. IX part 2, pp. 2020-2021; *Dialogo e Annuncio*, no. 28.

44 Cfr. Ibid., no. 29.

45 Cfr. Ibid., no. 27.

4.5 Need for discernment and purification

Dialogue and Proclamation says that, to identify in other religions elements of grace capable of sustaining the positive response of their members to God's invitation is difficult, and so discernment is required. Besides, it does not follow that everything in them is good[46] and result of grace, because sin has been at work in the world, and so religious traditions reflect limitations of the human spirit. In addition, an open and positive approach to other religions cannot overlook the contradictions which may exist between them and Christian revelation, and the incompatibility between some fundamental elements of Christianity and some aspects of non-Christian religions.[47] Therefore, while entering with an open mind into dialogue with the followers of other religions, Christians may have also to challenge them in a peaceful spirit with regard to the content of their belief. But Christians too must allow themselves to be questioned, because notwithstanding the fullness of God's revelation in Christ, the way Christians sometimes understand their religion and practice it, might be in need of purification.[48]

5. Place of interreligious dialogue in the evangelising mission of the Church

The second part of *Dialogue and Proclamation* deals with the place of interreligious dialogue in the evangelising mission of the Church. For this, it is important to know the kind of ecclesiology which the document proposes.

5.1 Ecclesiology of Dialogue and Proclamation

The ecclesiology of *Dialogue and Proclamation* is drawn basically from Vatican II which affirms that, the Church has been willed by God and instituted by Christ to be the sign and instrument of the divine plan of salvation (*LG* 1), it is the universal sacrament of salvation

46 Cfr. Ibid., no. 30.

47 Cfr. Ibid., no. 31.

48 Cfr. Ibid., no. 32.

(*LG* 48), it is necessary for salvation (*LG* 14), and Jesus himself inaugurated the mission of the Church by preaching the coming of God's Kingdom (*LG* 5).[49] Though principally, this Kingdom is revealed in the person of Christ himself, the Church on earth is the 'seed and the beginning' of that Kingdom. Thus, the Kingdom is inseparable from the Church, because both are inseparable from the person and work of Christ, and consequently it is not possible to separate the Church from the Kingdom.[50] The Church on earth is also always on pilgrimage[51] and constantly advancing towards the plenitude of divine truth.[52]

5.2 Religious traditions and the Church

Dialogue and Proclamation affirms that the members of other religions inasmuch as they respond to God's calling, as perceived by their conscience, are saved in Jesus Christ, and thus already share in some way in the reality which is signified by the Kingdom.[53] Since the mission of the Church is to foster the Kingdom of Christ, part of her role consists in recognizing that the inchoate reality of this Kingdom can be found *also beyond the confines of the Church*, for example, in the hearts of the followers of other religions, insofar as they live evangelical values and are open to the action of the Spirit. Nevertheless, it must be remembered that this is an inchoate reality, which needs to find completion through being related to the Kingdom of Christ already present in the Church, yet realized fully only in the world to come.[54]

49 Cfr. Ibid., no. 33.

50 Cfr. *Insegnamenti di Giovanni Paolo II*, Vol. XII part 1, Città del Vaticano, Libreria Editrice Vaticana, 1991, pp. 748-749.

51 Cfr. *Dialogo e Annuncio*, no. 36.

52 Cfr. Ibid., no. 37.

53 Cfr. Ibid., no. 35.

54 Cfr. Ibid.

5.3 Dialogue of salvation

The foundation of the Church's commitment to dialogue is not merely anthropological but primarily theological. As taught by Pope Paul VI[55] and Pope John Paul II[56], it is a dialogue of salvation, even as God has entered into an age-old dialogue of salvation with humankind which is continued even today. In faithfulness to the divine initiative, the Church too must enter into a dialogue of salvation with all peoples. This makes interreligious dialogue an integral element of the Church's evangelizing mission.[57]

5.4 Dialogue as invitation to deeper religious commitment

In dialogue of salvation, Christians and others are called to collaborate with the Spirit who is universally present and active. Interreligious dialogue does not merely aim at mutual understanding and friendly relations. It reaches a much deeper level, that of the spirit, where exchange and sharing consist in a mutual witness to one's beliefs and a common exploration of one's respective religious convictions. In dialogue, Christians and others are invited to deepen their religious commitment, to respond with increasing sincerity to God's personal call and self-gift which always passes through the mediation of Jesus Christ and the work of his Spirit.[58]

5.5 Dialogue as deeper conversion to God

The aim of interreligious dialogue is a deeper conversion of all towards God, and as such it possesses its own validity. In this process, decision may be made by someone to leave one's previous spiritual or religious situation in order to direct oneself towards another.[59] Dialogue implies mutual acceptance of differences, or even of contradictions,

55 Cfr. Paul VI, *Ecclesiam suam*, no. 72, p. 642.

56 Cfr. *Insegnamenti di Giovanni Paolo II*, Vol. VII part 1, Citta del Vaticano, Libreria Editrice Vaticana, 1984 1984, p. 598; *Dialogo e Annuncio*, no. 39.

57 Cfr. *Dialogo e Annuncio*, no. 38.

58 Cfr. Ibid., no. 40.

59 Cfr. Ibid., no. 41; *Dialogo e Missione*, no. 37.

and respect for the free decision of persons according to the dictates of their conscience.[60] This is because, "All men are bound to seek the truth, especially in what concerns God and his Church, and to embrace it and to hold on to it as they come to know it."[61]

6. Forms of dialogue

Dialogue and Proclamation reproduces in summary form the four forms of interreligious dialogue already dealt with in *Dialogue and Mission* with a brief explanation on each of them. They are: *dialogue of life*, *dialogue of action*, *dialogue of theological exchange*, and *dialogue of religious experience*[62], without claiming to establish among them any order of priority. The document also affirms that there is an interdependence of the various forms of dialogue. It further says that all are called to dialogue, though not all in the same way.[63]

7. Importance of interreligious dialogue

The document highlights the urgency and importance of interreligious dialogue for the following reasons:

7.1 Dialogue for human liberation

The document stresses the importance of dialogue for integral development, social justice and human liberation. Local Churches are called upon to commit themselves in this respect in an unselfish and impartial manner. There is need to stand up for human rights, to promote justice, and to denounce injustice not only when their own members are victimized, but independently of the religious allegiance of the victims. There is need also to join together in trying

---

60 Cfr. *Dignitatis Humane*, no. 2.

61 Ibid., no. 1.

62 Cfr. *Dialogo e Annuncio*, no. 42; *Dialogo e Missione*, nos. 29-35. There are two minor terminological changes: 'dialogue of works' is changed to 'dialogue of action', and 'dialogue of experts' is changed to 'dialogue of theological exchange'.

63 Cfr. *Dialogo e Annuncio*, no. 43.

to solve the great problems facing society and the world, as well as in education for justice and peace.[64]

7.2 Dialogue with culture

Dialogue and Proclamation affirms that culture is a context in which interreligious dialogue seems urgent. Culture is broader than religion, and there exists a complex relationship between the two. It can be said that religion represents the transcendent dimension of culture, and in a certain way its soul. Religions have definitely contributed to the progress of culture and the construction of a more humane society. Yet religious practices have sometimes had an alienating influence upon cultures. An autonomous secular culture can play a critical role with regard to some negative elements in particular religions. Several religions may co-exist within one and the same cultural framework, and conversely, the same religion may find expression in different cultural contexts. Again, religious differences may lead to distinct cultures in the same region.[65]

Christianity supports many values found and lived in the rich heritage of cultures, but it may also challenge certain culturally accepted values. True dialogue implies recognizing and accepting cultural values which respect human dignity and transcendent destiny. It may happen, that some aspects of traditional Christian cultures are challenged by the local cultures of other religious traditions.[66]

7.3 Dialogue to eliminate tensions and conflicts

Interreligious dialogue at cultural level can eliminate tensions and conflicts, and potential confrontations by a better understanding among the various religious cultures of a given region. It may contribute to purifying cultures from dehumanizing elements, and thus be an agent of transformation of culture. It can also help to uphold certain traditional cultural values which are under threat

64 Cfr. Ibid., no. 44.

65 Cfr. Ibid., no. 45.

66 Cfr. Ibid., no. 46. Nowhere in *Dialogue and Proclamation* culture is defined. The emphasis here seems to be on the 'dialectics' between culture and religion.

from modernity, and the levelling down which indiscriminate internationalization may bring with it.[67]

8. Dispositions for Interreligious Dialogue

The document discusses in some detail, the dispositions required for interreligious dialogue, and they are the following:

8.1 A balanced attitude

Dialogue requires on the part of Christians as well as of the followers of other religions, a balanced attitude which avoids the extremes of a certain ingenuousness which accepts everything, without further questioning, and a hypercritical attitude which leads to suspicion. A balanced attitude means openness and receptivity towards others, overcoming prejudices, unselfishness and impartiality, and accepting differences and possible contradictions, commitment to truth and willingness to allow oneself to be transformed by the encounter.[68] To this, Michael Fitzgerald adds that, there should be respect, and should not embarrass people by inviting them to say words or perform gestures with which they are not comfortable.[69]

8.2 Strong conviction about one's religious faith

Dialogue demands from the partners a strong conviction about their respective religious faiths.[70] Without this there would be a danger of indifference to religious values. If one's own beliefs are not strong enough, a challenge might lead to a defensive or even aggressive attitude.[71] For Christians, this strong conviction would mean a firm

---

67 Cfr. Ibid., no. 46. Here, the reference seems to be to 'globalization', but the document avoids the term, probably due to its complexity and the difficulty in defining it. Another term the document seems to avoid is 'postmodernity' probably due to its ambiguity.

68 Cfr. Ibid., no. 47; Michael L. Fitzgerald and John Borelli, *Interfaith Dialogue* p. 168.

69 Cfr. Ibid., p. 34.

70 Cfr. *Dialogo e Annuncio*, no. 48.

71 Cfr. Michael L. Fitzgerald and John Borelli, *Interfaith Dialogue,* p. 34.

belief that Jesus Christ is Son of God and saviour, and the only mediator between God and man (1 Tm 2:4-6), and that he is the fullness of revelation (Heb 1:1). But Christians must remember that God has also manifested himself in some way to the followers of other religions. Consequently, it is with receptive minds that they approach the convictions and values of others.[72]

8.3 Openness to truth

Openness to truth is another disposition needed for dialogue. For Christians, the fullness of truth is revealed in Jesus Christ. But *Dialogue and Proclamation* asks the Christians to remember that this fact does not give individual Christians the guarantee that they have grasped that truth fully, because grasping the truth is an unending process. Therefore, while keeping their identity intact, Christians must be prepared to learn and to receive from and through others, the positive values of their traditions. Through dialogue they may be led to give up ingrained prejudices, revise preconceived ideas, and even sometimes allow the understanding of their faith to be purified.[73] Openness towards others leads to the admission that the whole of the truth is not just on one side. There is always a need to learn from others, to receive from them, to benefit from their values and everything that is good in their traditions.[74]

Fitzgerald adds some further dispositions for dialogue, such as: a) a *contemplative spirit* through which one is able to discover and admire what God is doing through the Spirit, in the world and in the lives of people; b) *prayer* which is a dialogue with God and which provides a solid foundation for dialogue; and c) *patience and perseverance* because one cannot look for quick results in dialogue.[75]

72 Cfr. *Dialogo e Annuncio*, no. 48.

73 Cfr. Ibid., no. 49.

74 Cfr. Michael L. Fitzgerald and John Borelli, *Interfaith Dialogue*, p. 169.

75 Cfr. Ibid., p. 35.

9. Fruits of dialogue

Dialogue and Proclamation says that if Christians cultivate openness towards other religions, and allow themselves to be tested, they will be able to gather the fruits of dialogue (which can also be considered as goals of dialogue). The first fruit is the ability to discover with admiration all that God has accomplished through Jesus Christ in his Spirit, and continues to accomplish in the world, and in the whole of humankind. Secondly, dialogue will deepen their Christian faith, and will become increasingly aware of their Christian identity, and perceive more clearly the distinctive elements of the Christian message. Thirdly they will discover the active presence of the mystery of Jesus Christ beyond the visible boundaries of the Church and of the Christian fold.[76]

According to Dupuis, the real fruit of dialogue intended by the document is a common conversion (*metanoia*) of Christians and the members of other religions to the same God.[77] Fitzgerald says that mutual understanding and mutual enrichment are important fruits of dialogue.[78] Jose Kuttianimattathil avers that, dialogue gives the partners a greater knowledge of each other and of each other's religious traditions, and thus helps them to overcome prejudices, misinformation and negative attitudes. This in turn leads to a greater acceptance of each other with their religious traditions. It also helps one to purify one's faith, and enrich one's beliefs, and submit their lives more generously to God and to the service of others. Thus, dialogue leads to conversion, which in certain cases can lead to the acceptance of a new religious community.[79] To this one may add that, dialogue can have also positive effects in civil society at national and intentional levels, especially with regards to human rights,

76 Cfr. *Dialogo e Annuncio*, no. 50.

77 Cfr. Jacques Dupuis, *Toward a Christian Theology of Religious Pluralism,* p. 383.

78 Cfr. Michael L. Fitzgerald and John Borelli, *Interfaith Dialogue,* p. 28.

79 Cfr. Jose Kuttianimattathil, *Practice and Theology of Interreligious Dialogue,* Bangalore, Kristu Jyoti Publications, 1998, pp. 589-591.

religious freedom, and promotion of world peace and peace between religions.

10. Obstacles to dialogue

Dialogue and Proclamation speaks of several obstacles to dialogue, some of which can be applied equally to the members of all religions, while others may affect some religions more specifically and make it difficult to initiate dialogue. Some of the important obstacles are the following: a*)* insufficient grounding in one's own faith; b*)* insufficient knowledge and understanding of the belief and practices of other religions; c) cultural differences arising from different levels of instruction or from the use of different languages; d*)* socio-political factors or some burdens of the past; e*)* wrong understanding of the meaning of terms such as conversion, baptism, dialogue, etc. f*)* self-sufficiency, and lack of openness leading to defensive or aggressive attitudes; g*)* a lack of conviction with regard to the value of interreligious dialogue, which some may see as a task reserved to specialists, and others as a sign of weakness or even a betrayal of the faith; h*)* suspicion about the other's motives in dialogue; i*)* a polemical spirit when expressing religious convictions; j*)* intolerance, which is often aggravated by association with political, economic, racial and ethnic factors, and a lack of reciprocity in dialogue which can lead to frustration; and k*)* certain features of the present religious climate, such as growing materialism, religious indifference, and the multiplication of religious sects which creates confusion and raises new problems.[80]

Dialogue and Proclamation says that many of these obstacles arise from a lack of understanding of the true nature and goal of interreligious dialogue. Obviously much patience is required to practice dialogue. The Church's commitment to dialogue is not dependent on success in achieving mutual understanding and enrichment, rather it flows from God's initiative in entering into a dialogue with humankind, and from the example of Jesus Christ.[81]

80 Cfr. *Dialogo e Annuncio*, no. 52.

81 Cfr. Ibid., no. 53.

The document further says that, the obstacles, though real, should not lead to underestimate the possibilities of dialogue, or to overlook the results already achieved. There has been a growth in mutual understanding, and in active co-operation due to dialogue. Dialogue has had a positive impact on the Church itself. Other religions have also been led through dialogue to renewal and greater openness. Dialogue has also made it possible for the Church to share Gospel values with followers of other religions. Hence the document affirms: "So despite the difficulties, the Church's commitment to dialogue remains firm and irreversible."[82] Fitzgerald, who has much experience in dialogue, adds that, in interreligious dialogue one cannot expect immediate results. There is a need to prepare the ground, build up confidence and establish friendship so that relationships can grow stronger. One has to be patient and persevere in hope, and fruit will certainly come in due time.[83]

11. Relationship between dialogue and proclamation

The third part of *Dialogue and Proclamation* is dedicated to a discussion on the relationship between interreligious dialogue and proclamation.[84] It is an attempt to resolve the problem of the 'conflict' between dialogue and proclamation, which was one of the important aims of the document.

---

82 *Dialogue and Proclamation*, no. 54. The quotations in English in this chapter are taken from the official English translation of *Dialogo e Annuncio* available with Pontifical Council for Interreligious Dialogue: "Dialogue and Proclamation. Reflection and Orientations on Interreligious Dialogue and the Proclamation of the Gospel of Jesus Christ ", in *Interreligious Dialogue. The Official Teaching of the Catholic Church from the Second Vatican Council to John Paul II (1963-2005)*, Francesco Gioia (ed.), Boston, Pauline Books and Media, 2006, 1156-1189.

83 Cfr. Michael L. Fitzgerald and John Borelli, *Interfaith Dialogue*, p. 12.

84 The second part of *Dialogue and Proclamation* (articles 55-77) is fully dedicated to a discussion on proclamation of the message of Jesus Christ. Since our main concern is with interreligious dialogue, we shall not discuss it.

11.1 Interrelated but not interchangeable

Dialogue and Proclamation clearly affirms that, though dialogue and proclamation are both authentic elements of the Church's one evangelising mission, they are not on the same level. It is true that both are legitimate, necessary, and intimately related, but they are not interchangeable. Both dialogue and proclamation remain as two distinct activities of the Church, but one and the same local Church, and one and the same person, can be diversely engaged in both.[85]

11.2 Awareness of circumstances, sensitivity and dialogical spirit

Dialogue and Proclamation states that, in the concrete way of fulfilling the mission of the Church, one should be attentive to the particular circumstances, and manifest sensitivity to the social, cultural, religious and political situation, and attentiveness to the signs of the times. This sensitivity and attentiveness is developed through a spirituality of dialogue which requires a prayerful discernment and theological reflection on the plan of God for the various religions, and the experience of those who find in them their spiritual nourishment.[86] One who proclaims should practice dialogue in proclamation because the hearer of the Word is not expected to be a passive receiver.[87] Besides, a 'dialogical spirit' should animate all the activities related to the evangelising mission of the Church.

11.3 Companions on common path

The Church's mission is extended to all people, and in the process it will come into contact with followers of other religions. *Dialogue and Proclamation* says that the Church in dialogue with other religions has a prophetic role. In bearing witness to the Gospel and it raises questions to them, but it may also find itself challenged in turn. So the members of the Church and the followers of other religions find themselves to be companions on the common path which humanity

85 Cfr. *Dialogo e Annuncio*, no. 77.

86 Cfr. Ibid., no. 78.

87 Cfr. Ibid., no. 70.

is called to tread.[88] This was especially highlighted by Pope John Paul II in 1986 in Assisi when he described the history of humanity to be: "a fraternal journey in which we accompany one another towards the transcendental goal which he [God] sets before us."[89]

11.4 Dialogue cannot replace proclamation

Dialogue and Proclamation clearly states that, dialogue cannot replace proclamation. Proclamation and dialogue are two different ways of carrying out the one mission of the Church, and all Christians are called to be personally involved in both proclamation and dialogue. But dialogue does not constitute the whole mission of the Church, and it cannot simply replace proclamation, but it remains oriented towards proclamation, in so far as the dynamic process of the Church's evangelising mission reaches in it its climax and fullness.[90] But proclamation is to be carried out in full respect for freedom.[91]

11.5 Reciprocity and openness to the promptings of the Spirit

Dialogue and Proclamation affirms that, for Christians, dialogue consists in sharing with others their joy in knowing and following Jesus Christ. The followers of other religions should also desire sincerely to share their faith. This implies that, all dialogue implies reciprocity, and aims at banishing fear and aggressiveness.[92] Christians must be prepared to follow the promptings of the Spirit in proclamation, witness and dialogue. Therefore, all those who are involved in dialogue are invited by God himself to seek his light and

88 Cfr. Ibid., no. 79.

89 *Insegnamenti di Giovanni Paolo II*, 1986 Vol. IX, part 2, p. 1262.

90 Cfr. *Dialogo e Annuncio*, no. 82. There are theologians who disagree with this. For example for Paul F. Knitter mission *is* dialogue whereby evangelisation is simply reduced to dialogue and the witness to one's faith dialogue implies. He thus does away with proclamation as a distinct expression of evangelisation. Cfr. Paul F. Knitter, *Jesus and Other Names. Christian Mission and Global Responsibility*, New York, Orbis Books, 1996, pp. 142-147.

91 Cfr. *Dialogo e Annuncio*, no. 84.

92 Cfr. Ibid., no. 83.

truth, and only God knows the times and stages of the fulfilment of this long human quest.[93]

11.6 Jesus as model in dialogue and proclamation

Dialogue and Proclamation presents Jesus as the model and guide in the commitment to both proclamation and dialogue.[94] Christians are not only to imitate him, but also to be closely united to him through prayer, especially the Eucharist. It is here that they draw the grace of discernment to be able to read the signs of the Spirit's presence, and to recognize the favourable time and right manner of proclaiming Christ.[95]

11.7 Dialogue is also for other religions

The Church encourages and fosters interreligious dialogue also for non-Christian religions, and among themselves. It invites all religious institutions and movements to meet, to enter into dialogue and collaboration, and to purify themselves in order to promote truth and life, holiness, justice, love and peace, which are dimensions of the Kingdom of God to come. In this way, interreligious dialogue truly becomes part of the dialogue of salvation initiated by God.[96]

11.8 Other teachings

The document says that, since religions differ from one another, special attention is to be given to relations with the followers of each religion.[97] Specific studies are to be undertaken on the relationship between dialogue and proclamation, and in the light of these studies, special courses and study sessions could be organised to train people for both dialogue and proclamation. Attention is to be given to

93 Cfr. Ibid., no. 84.

94 Cfr. Ibid., no. 85.

95 Cfr. Ibid., no. 86.

96 Cfr. Ibid., no. 80. See also *Insegnamenti di Giovanni Palo II,* Vol. VII part 1, p. 598.

97 Cfr. *Dialogo e Annuncio*, no. 87.

young people living in a pluralistic environment, where they meet the followers of other religions at school, at work, in youth movements and other associations, and even within their own families.[98] All Christians, according to their situation, should be encouraged to equip themselves to fulfil the two-fold commitment of dialogue and proclamation. Finally, dialogue and proclamation are more than tasks to be accomplished, graces to be sought in prayer, and therefore, one should continually implore the help of the Holy Spirit.[99]

12. A critical appreciation

Dialogue and Proclamation is a faithful reflection and careful application of the teachings of Vatican II and the subsequent magisterium on interreligious dialogue, especially of Pope John Paul II. It builds upon and compliments *Dialogue and Mission* of 1984. In this sense, it can be considered as the most updated document currently available in the Catholic Church on interreligious dialogue.

The document highlights the new awareness of the fact of religious pluralism, and presents an overall positive view of non-Christian religions. A delicate balance is achieved in the relationship between dialogue and proclamation, and their specific identity and complementarity are spelt out. Though the document deals with dialogue *and* proclamation, its emphasis is clearly on interreligious dialogue, but without undermining the ontological priority of proclamation over dialogue.

Dialogue and Proclamation invokes a fourfold theological foundation for interreligious dialogue: a) the common origin and the single destiny of the human race in God (Anthropological), b) universal salvation in Jesus Christ (Christological), c) the active presence and action of the Holy Spirit in the world (Pneumatological), and d) the universality of the Reign of God (Kingdomcentric ecclesiology). According to Dupuis, from the theological perspective, the fourth

98 Cfr. Ibid., no. 88.

99 Cfr. Ibid., no. 89.

view goes beyond Vatican II, and constitutes the deepest foundation for interreligious dialogue.[100]

Dialogue and Proclamation teaches that, the members of other religions are saved by Jesus Christ 'in the sincere practice of what is good in their religious traditions'. According to Dupuis, this is a weighty statement and whose theological import must not be underestimated. It means, in effect that, the members of other religions are not saved by Christ in spite of or beside their own traditions but *in them*, and in some mysterious way 'known to God', *through them.* He adds that, if further elaborated theologically, this statement would be seen to imply some hidden presence – no matter how imperfect – of the mystery of Jesus Christ in these religions in which salvation reaches their adherents.[101] But it must be added that, there is no blanket approval of other religions, and the document never puts them on a par with the One, Holy, Catholic and Apostolic Church. Other religions can provide help along the way of salvation, but they are not independent ways of salvation.

Dialogue and Proclamation introduces some novelties in the text: it speaks of dialogue in the context of culture, makes reference to obstacles to dialogue, to dispositions needed for dialogue, the importance of sensitivity to the particularity of each religion, and the need for specialised studies on dialogue and proclamation.

The document affirms that sincerity in dialogue requires that each enters into it with the integrity of his or her own faith. According to Dupuis, this statement lays to rest the contention made by some in recent years that putting aside (practicing an *epochè*) – at least provisionally – faith in Jesus Christ as the universal saviour is, on the Christian side, a pre-required condition for entering into dialogue, and a test of the sincerity of the dialogue itself.[102]

---

100 Cfr. Jacques Dupuis, *Toward a Christian Theology of Religious Pluralism,* pp. 346, 358.

101 Cfr. Jacques Dupuis, "A Theological Commentary: Dialogue and Proclamation", p. 137.

102 Cfr. Ibid., p. 140. For a good analysis of the problem of *epochè* see Jose Kuttianimattathil, *Practice and Theology of Interreligious Dialogue,* pp. 477-483.

The relationship between dialogue and proclamation is a topic which might be of interest also for other religions in as much as proclamation is practiced not only a Christianity but also by other faiths. For example, Buddhism and Islam are clearly missionary religions right from their inception, and strongly believe in the importance, necessity, urgency and value of proclamation. Even in religions like Hinduism, Jainism, Judaism, Confucianism, the concept of proclamation is not absent, though it does not play a central role. A similar thing can be said of many other religions.

Regarding the weaknesses of the document, Fitzgerald says that, it is in need of a better biblical theology of religions, a more comprehensive treatment of the teachings and practice of dialogue in the Church down through the ages (both positive and negative), and a greater emphasis on the anthropological basis for interreligious dialogue.[103]

Dupuis points out that the document is not free from ambiguities. He asks: if proclamation needs to be present always, is dialogue *in itself* a genuine form of evangelisation? Can it be maintained that both are absolutely necessary?[104] He also points out that, *Dialogue and Proclamation* while affirming after Vatican II, the necessity of the Church as universal, enters no further into the question *how* this necessity applies, and how the Church is operative in the salvation of people outside.[105]

Though the document deals with culture, its complexity is bypassed. One may ask if religion is the 'transcendent dimension of culture' as *Dialogue and Proclamation* claims, how is it that some cultures reject religion or will not allow entry of missionaries or forbid conversion as a rejection and betrayal of one's own culture?

---

103 Cfr. Michael L. Fitzgerald, "A Theological Reflection on Interreligious Dialogue", in *Catholic Engagement with World Religions. A Comprehensive Study*, Karl Josef Becker and Ilaria Morali (eds.), New York, Orbis Books, 2010, pp. 389-390.

104 Cfr. Jacques Dupuis, *Toward a Christian Theology of Religious Pluralism*, pp. 370-371.

105 Cfr. Jacques Dupuis, "A Theological Commentary: Dialogue and Proclamation", pp. 138-139.

Dialogue and Proclamation does not introduce anything new in the forms of dialogue but simply reproduces in summary form what was already said by *Dialogue and Mission*. The fruits of dialogue are somewhat scattered through the document, and the discussion on it seems to lack comprehensiveness. Among the many obstacles to dialogue, one does not find any mention being made to religious fundamentalism which is a real threat to dialogue today. Ecumenical dimension in interreligious dialogue and the contribution of the laity in dialogue have not received the attention they deserve.

It is true that *Dialogue and Proclamation* attempts to 'solve' the conflict between dialogue and proclamation, but in the practical life of many local Churches and Christians, integrating the two is still a major problem. Experience shows that, where dialogue is well founded, proclamation is relativized, and where proclamation flourishes, dialogue takes a back seat. In this sense the document appears to be quite idealistic.

13. Conclusion

Dialogue and Proclamation is undoubtedly the most comprehensive, theologically well-founded and forward-looking document of the Catholic Church on interreligious dialogue. Its major merit consists in providing a clarification on the relationship between dialogue and proclamation, and 'solving' the conflict between the two, at least from the theoretical point of view. The document presents interreligious dialogue as an essential dimension of the Church's mission, and reaffirms its validity and necessity. It emphatically states that the commitment of the Church to interreligious dialogue is irreversible. Nevertheless, in many contexts, even after the publication of important documents on dialogue like, *Ecclesiam suam, Nostra aetate*, *Dialogue and Mission* and *Dialogue and Proclamation*, and the untiring efforts of the Pontifical Council for Interreligious Dialogue to promote dialogue, some have barely began to 'scratch the surface' of interreligious dialogue. Local Churches and its leaders, seminaries, Christian educational institutions and organisations need to make greater efforts to make the content of these documents better known and implemented, and Christians are formed according to their spirit and principles. One should also critically examine the methods used in dialogue.[106] These seem to be the biggest challenges before the Catholic Church today with regard to interreligious dialogue.

106 In this context, Jose Kuttianimattathil's reflections on the future of dialogue, and the suggestions he makes to take it forward, seems to be very useful. See Jose Kuttianimattathil, *Practice and Theology of Interreligious Dialogue*, pp. 612-635.

Chapter 6

The Current State of Interreligious Dialogue

Today there is a growing awareness among many Catholics that interreligious dialogue is an essential dimension of the mission of the Church in the contemporary world. In fact, it is one of the important concerns of the Catholic Church since the promulgation of the Declaration *Nostra aetate.* Prior to that, as we have already seen, Pope Paul VI, through his encyclical *Ecclesiam suam* had asked the Catholics to enter into dialogue with the entire humanity: with separated Christians, believers, non-Christians and even atheists. Interreligious dialogue is also an important element in the magisterium of the Popes since the Vatican II. Dialogue is an invitation to go beyond mere co-existence or tolerance of other religions to active engagement with them in a spirit of friendship and brotherhood in order to develop a deep level of communion between religious persons and communities. The Catholic Church engages in dialogue because it is the method of conversation which God himself chose to communicate with humanity.

1. The activities of the Pontifical Council for Interreligious Dialogue (PCID)

The Pontifical Council for Interreligious Dialogue is the special structure within the Catholic Church that is responsible for promoting interreligious relations. From 1964 to 1988 it was known as the Secretariat for Non-Christians. On 29 June 1988 in the Apostolic Constitution on the Roman Curia entitled "Pastor Bonus" Pope John Paul II renamed the Secretariat as 'Pontifical Council for Interreligious Dialogue' and specified its main activities, and its relationship with other departments of the Roman Curia.[1] The Council encourages all Catholics, the local Churches, followers of other religions, people gifted with some religious sense, and all people of good will, to engage in interreligious dialogue. It promotes mutual understanding, respect and collaboration between Catholics and the followers of other religions, scientific study of other religions, inculturation, gives advice on the way dialogue is to be practiced, and assists the formation of persons dedicated to dialogue.[2] It welcomes visitors from local Churches and representatives of other religions to its central office in Rome for dialogue and common reflection on relevant themes. These meetings are either bilateral or multilateral. The president[3] and the secretary of the Council frequently travel to

1 Cfr. *Insegnamenti di Giovanni Paolo II*, Vol. XI part 2, Citta del Vaticano, Libreria Editrice Vaticana, 1989, pp. 2321; 2394.

2 Cfr. Michael L. Fitzgerald and John Borelli, *Interfaith Dialogue,* p. 240; http://www.vatican.va/roman_curia/pontifical_councils/interelg/documents/rc_pc_interelg_pro_20051996_en.html (23.2.2015).

3 The current president of the Council is Jean-Louis Cardinal Tauran (2007-). Other presidents were: Paolo Cardinal Marella (1964-1973); Sergio Cardinal Pignedoli (1973-1980); Archbishop Jean Jadot (1980-1984); Francis Cardinal Arinze (1984-2002) Archbishop Michael L. Fitzgerald (2002-2006); Paul Cardinal Poupard (2006-2007). Cfr. Michael L. Fitzgerald and John Borelli, *Interfaith Dialogue,*p p. 239-240. http://en.wikipedia.org/wiki/Pontifical_Council_for_Interreligious_Dialogue (24.3.2015).

meet the representatives and leaders of other religions in different counties and cultural settings for dialogue and exchange of views. The Council has an ongoing relationship with the corresponding office in the World Council of Churches.[4]

The PCID has a decision-making body, an advisory body and an executive body. The decision-making body is composed of the members of the Council, about 30 in number, Cardinals and Bishops from different parts of the world. Every two or three years a plenary assembly is held in order to discuss important issues and to set guidelines for the work of the Council. The advisory body has about 50 members, called consultors, who are specialists in religious studies or in the practice of interreligious dialogue, residing in all continents. They assist the PCID through their research, information and suggestions. Periodically meetings of consultors are held, often on a continental level. The executive body consists of the permanent staff in Rome, made up of president, secretary, under-secretary, bureau chief for Islam, staff members for Africa and Asia, a staff member for New Religious Movements, an administrative assistant and support staff.[5]

The PCID does not have responsibility for dialogue between Christians and Jews. It is the competence of the Commission for Religious Relations with Jews, established in 1974, which comes under the Pontifical Council for Promoting Christian Unity. But it has a special Commission for Relations with Muslims, established in 1974, which is composed of a president, vice-president and secretary, and a small group of eight consultors. It engages in studies on different aspects of Christian-Muslim relations.[6]

The PCID assists the episcopal conferences and dioceses in promoting interreligious dialogue. There are meetings with bishops coming to Rome for their five-yearly *ad limina* visits, and with other groups of visitors. Periodically formal meetings are organised

4 Cfr. http://www.vatican.va/roman_curia/pontifical_councils/interelg/documents/rc_pc_interelg_pro_20051996_en.html (23.2.2015).

5 Cfr. Ibid.

6 Ibid.

for the Catholic leaders in order to encourage them in the way of dialogue. The Council carries out theological and pastoral reflections on interreligious dialogue with the help of experts, and they restrict themselves to religious questions and do not directly enter into socio-political issues. The ecumenical dimension of interreligious dialogue is also kept in mind in such reflections and encounters. The PCID addresses peoples of other religions yearly on the occasion of a religious celebration of particular importance to the religion in question. It publishes a journal, three times a year, called *Pro Dialogo* (previously called *Bulletin*) containing significant Church texts on dialogue, articles, and news of dialogue activities throughout the world. The Council usually publishes the Acts of the dialogue meetings it organizes.[7] It also periodically publishes monographs on world religions and themes related to dialogue. In 1993 the *Nostra aetate* Foundation was established by the PCID whose main purpose is to provide scholarship for students belonging to other religions who wish to improve their knowledge of Christianity by studying in one of the Pontifical academies or universities of Rome.[8]

Over the years much has been achieved in the field of interreligious relations all over the world, thanks to the untiring work of the PCID and its corresponding commissions in the episcopal conferences in various countries, regions and dioceses. From the yearly report which the Council presents to the Holy See on its activities, one can get an overview of its activities with leaders and representatives of other religions, both in Rome and in different parts of the world. Commenting on the initiatives promoted by the PCID and the responses received, Cardinal Cassidy says: "Beginning practically from scratch, the church has been able to establish relations with representatives of all the major world religions. Barriers have been broken down, misunderstandings corrected, and a new spirit of tolerance and trust created."[9]

7 Ibid.

8 Cfr. Michael L. Fitzgerald and John Borelli, *Interfaith Dialogue*, p. 241.

9 Edward Idris Cassidy, *Ecumenism and Interreligious Dialogue*, p. 225.

2. Situation of interreligious dialogue in local churches

The magisterium of the Church has always insisted that interreligious dialogue has an important place in the pastoral activities of the local Churches, and has given clear guidelines on how to carry it out. Hence the local Churches have the duty to promote interreligious dialogue because it is one of the important ways of carrying out the mission of the Church in the world. All the baptised persons are called upon to participate in dialogue, each one according to his or her capacity and state in life. In the local Churches the candidates to priestly and religious life, all catechists and lay leaders and collaborators in the mission are to become effective promoters of interreligious dialogue, because they share a responsibility with all Christians for fostering understanding and trust with members of other religions. Today in most Catholic dioceses there is a commission for the promotion of interreligious dialogue, but its way of functioning and the importance it gives to dialogue varies from diocese to diocese. In some dioceses these commissions are very active while in others they exist only in name. The same is the case with most Catholic parishes. In some parishes the commission for dialogue frequently organises interreligious encounters while in others such activities are practically non-existent. There are hardworking parish priests dedicated to dialogue but there are also pastors who show little interest in it. Among many Catholics there is still a widespread belief that dialogue is an activity reserved only for theologians and religious leaders. In many cases Catholics do not have adequate formation to interreligious dialogue. In most dioceses and parishes the involvement of the laity in dialogue is marginal. But certain charismatic individuals and groups carry forward the mission of interreligious dialogue with much success and fruitfulness when in the official Church dialogue takes a back seat in its pastoral life. There are many interreligious centres, associations and academic institutions which periodically organise bilateral and multilateral interreligious dialogues. There are also dioceses, parishes and organisations that encourage ecumenical involvement in interreligious dialogue. In spite of all these, going by the general trend in Catholic dioceses and parishes, more needs to be done in order to impart knowledge regarding the value and importance of interreligious dialogue to Catholics, especially at the grass root level, and encourage them to engage in dialogue in a systematic way. Thus there are many challenges before the local Churches, all over the world, with regard to interreligious dialogue.

3. Situation of formation to dialogue

The Church insists that formation to interreligious dialogue is indispensable for all categories of Christians, from ordinary lay faithful to the religious leaders. This is needed to avoid facile syncretism or uncompromising polemic or the hidden agenda to convert the other to one's own religion at any cost. Though all are invited to engage in dialogue with followers of other religions, many of them lack due preparation for it. Often in the teaching of the Catholic catechism interreligious dialogue is hardly given importance. The educational institutions like schools, colleges, universities and similar centres have an important role in formation to interreligious dialogue. Unfortunately seldom they are utilised for dispelling ignorance and prejudice about other religions, for promoting mutual understanding and for imparting formation to dialogue. In many seminaries the subject of interreligious dialogue is taught as an academic subject only, and the students are not introduced to the practical ways of carrying out dialogue. Efforts are rarely made to identify, encourage, promote and form persons particularly gifted to engage in dialogue with other religions. Thus, formation to interreligious dialogue remains as another challenge before the Catholic Church.

4. Problems in interreligious dialogue

It must be admitted that there is opposition to interreligious dialogue from some quarters because it is interpreted as promotion of relativism and betrayal of one's religious faith. Instead of dialogue they prefer to encourage exclusivism or opposition to other religions. Thus to make 'war' on religions becomes their policy. The religious fundamentalists can be considered as coming under this category.

There are people who ask whether it is possible to hold an absolutist view of the truthfulness of one's own religion[10] and still engage in an open dialogue with other religions. Certainly, no committed religious practitioner chooses relativism. But dialogue can lead to better understanding of one's own religion even if an absolutist position is held.

Some are opposed to dialogue because there is a fear that if one comes into frequent contact with other religions, there is the danger that one may end up in religious *relativism* believing that one religion is as good as another. Another fear is that contact with other religions can lead to religious *syncretism* which is an effort to put several religions together in order to create a 'new religion' of one's own. There are religious people who fear that if they encourage dialogue between religions some of their adherents may *seek better pastures elsewhere* as a result of their conviction that other religions have elements that can better satisfy their religious quests than one's own. Another fear is that if people are in constant contact with other religions some people can lose belief in any one religion and develop *religious indifference*.[11]

There are Christians who argue that the Church's mission *ad gentes* and interreligious dialogue cannot go together. If dialogue is practiced seriously, the proclamation of the Gospel will suffer, and this would go against the mandate of Christ to proclaim the Gospel to all creation (Mk 16:15). Some non-Christians criticise interreligious dialogue as a new method invented by the Catholic Church to proselytise. Non-Christians in general do not show much interest in dialogue, and there is lack of openness to dialogue on the part of many. Often the members of different religions are not sufficiently formed for dialogue.

No true interreligious dialogue is possible without religious liberty, and this is a major obstacle to dialogue in several countries

10 Religious absolutism is the assumption that, one's own religion is the only one that is divinely established, the only one that provides saving truths to all peoples, and the only one legitimate religion which should replace all others.

11 Cfr. Francis Arinze, *Meeting Other Believers*, pp. 18-21.

today. Healing historical memories of wars, conquests, defeats, conflicts, misunderstanding, hatred and prejudices is needed to initiate dialogue. When one engages in dialogue there are linguistic problems as the connotations of religious concepts can differ from religion to religion (for example, the use of such terms as, God, Absolute, revelation, incarnation, salvation, liberation, saviour, sin, faith, etc). Holding different theologies of religions can also create problems in dialogue. There are Catholics who have no serious engagement with their religion, and live a 'fully' secularised life, even if officially they are members of the Church. With such people no genuine interreligious dialogue is possible. Then there are Catholics who are sceptical about the future of interreligious dialogue.[12]

In recent years there has been an increasing interest in multiple religious belonging.[13] This is a tendency especially noticed in postmodernity. While the possibility of 'dual belonging' is contested the problem of dialogue remains. The question here is, can a person profess allegiance to different religions and yet engage in interreligious dialogue? The answer is that it may not be possible because rootedness in one's religion is one of the prerequisites for interreligious dialogue.

Too negative an attitude towards other religions is another obstacle to dialogue. In primitive Christianity openness to non-Christian religions was not widespread. For example, Clement of Alexandria (c. 150-215 A.D) was astonishingly hard on pagan religions. Speaking

12 For instance see Felix Wilfred, "Dialogue Gasping for Breath? Towards New Frontiers in Interreligious Dialogue", *Vidyajyoti*, 51 (October 1987), 449-466. John B. Chettimattam, "Editorial", *Jeevadhara,* 22 (September 1992), 328-330. An entire issue of *Jeevadhara* discussed the theme "Interreligious Dialogue in Crisis". Cfr. *Jeevadhara,* 22 (September 1992), 328-403. But Jose Kuttianimattahil, after having analysed these writings affirms that, contrary to the first impression, these authors are not arguing that dialogue does not have a future but rather pointing out certain pitfalls into which dialogue has been fallen and which have to be avoided as well as the steps that have to be taken so that dialogue can make its rightful contribution in a religiously pluralistic society. Cfr. Jose Kuttianimattahil, *Practice and Theology of Interreligious Dialogue,* pp. 612-613.

13 Cf. Paul Hedges, *Controversies in Interreligious Dialogue and the Theology of Religions,* London, SCM Press, 2010, pp. 91-92.

in the context of Greek pagan religions he said that they are steeped in superstition and ignorance, that they are human creations and subject to destruction, and that their deities are mere inventions of people who are under the power of Satan. Thus they have deviated from the truth by inventing gods and saviours for themselves.[14] Orthodox Protestantism holds a similar view. For example, the Protestant theologian Karl Barth (1886-1968) stated that all non-Christian religions are unbelief, an attempted replacement of the divine work by a human manufacture, and an effort of human beings to save themselves by their own forces. According to him, there is only one true religion, and that is Christianity.[15] Hendrick Kraemer (1888-1965) of the Dutch Reformed Church applied the Barthian position to missionary theology, and regarded non-Christian religions as a mere obstacle to good that must be entirely replaced by faith in Jesus Christ. Between Christianity and non-Christian religions there is no point of contact but only difference and antithesis.[16] Hence he argued that the Christian missionary approach should manifest "the fervent apostolic attitude that knows its commission to be to confront all peoples, societies and religions with the revelation in Christ as contained in Biblical realism, and entreat them to surrender in obedience to it."[17] Both Barth and Kraemer neglected the theories of *Logos Spermatikos* (Seminal Logos) and of *praeparatio evangelica* (Preparation for the Gospel) because, for them, such theories imply a negation of Christian revelation. Catholic theology since the last hundred years has maintained a less negative position. While the Church condemned pervasions in non-Christian religions like, pantheism, polytheism, idolatry, superstition, omens, incantation,

14 Cfr. Clement of Alexandria, *Exhortation to the Heathen* (*Protrepticus*), Philip Schaff *et al* (trs.) Memphis, Bottom of the Hill Publishing, 2012, chapters 1-IV, pp. 6-54.

15 Cfr. *Karl Barth: Church Dogmatics.* A Selection with Introduction by Helmut Gollwitzer, G.W. Bromiley (tr. and ed.), Edinburgh, T and T Clark, 1961, pp. 51-54.

16 Cfr.Hendrik Kramer, *The Christian Message in a Non-Christian World*, New York, Harper, 1938, p. 300.

17 Ibid., p. 343.

divination, etc., she did not deny the authentic human and religious values found in them. In fact, these values were interpreted as stepping stones to Christianity.

There are scholars and religious leaders who defend the traditional discipline of apologetics as an important component of interreligious relations. Thus they advocate not interreligious dialogue but interreligious apologetics.[18] According to them, a proper understanding of the status and importance of interreligious apologetics is essential to a clarification of the significance of religious claims to truth made in a context of radical religious pluralism.[19] Though the Catholic Church in the past had recourse to apologetics, it has moved away from it, and has opted for dialogue since the Vatican II. Hence we do not consider apologetics, in the strict sense, as part of interreligious dialogue. Here, the words of Raimon Panikkar is very apt: "Apologetics has its function and its proper place, but not here in the meeting of religions."[20]

5. Some theological models of interreligious dialogue

Currently there are many models of interreligious dialogue. The book *Introducing Theologies of Religions* by Paul Knitter discusses four major theological models on the relation of Christianity to non-Christian religions, which he names as, "Replacement Model", "Fulfilment Model", "Mutuality Model" and "Acceptance Model".[21] It seems to be a good presentation of the current major models, though not the only one, of interreligious dialogue. A brief explanation of them is given below:

18 See for example the work by Paul J. Griffiths, *An Apology for Apologetics. A Study in the Logic of Interreligious Dialogue,* New York, Orbis Books, 1991.

19 Cf. Ibid., p. 2.

20 Raimon Panikkar, *The Intrareligious Dialogue*, p. 26.

21 Cfr Paul Knitter, *Introducing Theologies of Religions*, New York, Maryknoll, 2008.

5.1 Replacement model

The "Replacement Model" maintains that, Christianity is the only true religion, and in the final analysis it is meant to replace all other religions. This model is represented especially by the so-called Fundamentalist or Evangelical Church communities.[22] Today they are split into four movements: Fundamentalists, Evangelicals, New Evangelicals, and Pentecostal or Charismatics.[23]

The Replacement Model takes two forms, total and partial. According to the *total* replacement theology, Christianity is the only true religion, and there is no value in other religions. Other religions are aberrant, and therefore Christianity must move in and take their place.[24] Many contemporary Fundamentalists, Evangelicals and Pentecostals hold this view. The *partial* replacement model is represented by New Evangelicals (moderate Evangelicals). They recognise general revelation of God in and through other religions, but *not salvation.* God does not save through other religions but only through Christ, and general revelation is insufficient as a vehicle for salvation.[25]

5.2 Fulfilment model

The "Fulfilment Model" offers a theology that tries to give equal weight to two fundamental Christian convictions: God's love is *universal* extending to all peoples, and Gods love is *particular* made real in Jesus Christ. This model is the general trend followed by the mainline Christian Churches like Roman Catholic, Greek Orthodox, Anglican, Lutheran, Reformed, Methodist, etc.[26]

The Fulfilment Model acknowledges the presence of truth and grace and the possibility of salvation in other religions.[27] But

22 Cfr Ibid., p. 19.

23 Cfr Ibid., p. 21.

24 Cfr Ibid., p. 23.

25 Cfr Ibid., pp. 33, 36.

26 Cfr Ibid., p. 63.

27 Cfr Ibid., p. 100.

it affirms that Christianity is the *true religion*, that Christ is the *one* and *only saviour* of all humanity, and it is non-negotiable.[28] Even if salvation may be possible for the followers of other religions through their own religions, it is through Christ alone that they are saved. This model is fundamentally Christ-centred and Church-centred, and the value of non-Christian religions consists in that they are a preparation for the Gospel.

5.3 Mutuality model

According to the "Mutuality Model", there are many true religions and all of them are called to dialogue, *as equals,* for mutual enrichment. Its underlying claim is that *Christianity is not the only true religion,* but there are also others, and Jesus of Nazareth cannot be presented as the one and only saviour of all because other religions also have similar savour figures.[29] God's universal love, presence and saving grace is found in all religions.[30] Since religions are different, there should be a relationship of mutuality between them, and should reciprocally open themselves to learning and self-transformation through dialogue. This Catholic Church does not accept this position.

5.4 Acceptance model

The "Acceptance Model" is the youngest of the models which grew up during the last two decades of the 20th century in the context of *postmodernism.* This model neither upholds the superiority of any one religion nor searches for a common something that makes them all valid, but *accepts the real diversity and particularity of all religions.*[31] Religions have *different ends* not just different means;[32] they speak *different languages;* they are all moving forward towards *different directions,* and since there are many religions there are also

---

28 Cfr Ibid., p. 103.

29 Cfr Ibid., p. 152.

30 Cfr Ibid., pp. 109, 111.

31 Cfr Ibid., p. 173.

32 Cfr Ibid., pp. 192-193.

many salvations[33], and multiplicity of Ultimates.[34] Since all religions are really different, relationship between them must be built on mutual acceptance, like good neighbours. Christians can speak of Christ as the only Son of God and only saviour of humanity, because it is the particular language of Christianity.[35] This does not mean that Christians deny salvation in other religions. There may be other channels of salvation of which Christianity knows nothing about. Dialogue is a good neighbour policy and its goal is not to attain a greater unity among religions but to maintain their diversity and learn from it.[36] This position is totally unacceptable to the Catholic Church.

Each of the four models discussed above has its own attractiveness and limitations, strengths and weaknesses. The *Replacement Model* upholds the core concerns of Christianity but is exclusive and aggressive, and negates the good in non-Christian religions. This can lead to feeling of superiority, disrespect, opposition, polemics, disagreement and unwillingness to engage in interreligious dialogue. The *Fulfilment Model* is absolutist because it claims that Christianity is the only true religion and other religions possess only partial truth. It affirms the uniqueness of Christ as the one and only saviour of humanity, which is central to Christian faith. The *Mutuality Model* is attractive as it can pave way for religious toleration and appreciation of the value of other religions, and promote dialogue better than replacement and fulfilment models. But it advocates relativism and waters down the uniqueness and centrality of Jesus Christ, which will not be acceptable to orthodox Christian faith. The *Acceptance Model* affirms the irreconcilable differences between religions and advocates absolute relativism. It is doubtful if this model can promote genuine dialogue as it denies any common ground or common language or commons symbols or common concerns among religions. Besides, it undermines the uniqueness of Jesus Christ, and speaks of many

33 Cfr Ibid.

34 Cfr Ibid., p. 194.

35 Cfr Ibid., p. 188.

36 Cfr Ibid., pp. 183, 220.

absolutes and many salvations, which is ontologically untenable. This is the most liberal and problematic of the four models. Among the four models suggested above, the *Fulfilment Model* seems to be more acceptable than the others, because it affirms the core concerns of the Replacement Model, and avoids the major limitations of the Mutuality Model and Acceptance Model, namely relativism and the downplaying or denial of the uniqueness of Christ.

6. Need for both interreligious and intercultural dialogue

A new trend that is emerging in the Catholic Church is to encourage both interreligious and intercultural dialogue, and one of its major proponents has been Pope Benedict XVI. Probably, he is among the few who understood the importance and necessity of *both* interreligious and intercultural of dialogue. He argued that, there is an intimate relationship between religion and culture, and genuine religion widens the horizons of human understanding, and stands at the foundation of any authentically human culture.[37] Besides, today, the possibilities of interaction between cultures have increased significantly, giving rise to new avenues for intercultural dialogue, and if such a dialogue is to be effective, it has to start from a deep knowledge of the specific identity of the various dialogue partners.[38] This would naturally mean taking seriously their respective cultures.

Though Pope Benedict XVI spoke of the importance of both intercultural and interreligious dialogue, he did not equate one with the other, because they refer to two different spheres, one religious and the other secular. Yet, he wanted them to interact with each other in a healthy way for the good of the human person and for common good. In fact, often he spoke of them as if they are two complementary aspects of one dialogue. Intercultural dialogue is important because it deepens the cultural consequences of basic religious ideas; interreligious dialogue is important because religion

37 Cfr. *Insegnamenti di Benedetto XVI,* Vol. V part 1, pp. 431, 791-793.

38 Cfr. Benedict XVI, *Caritas in veritate,* in *Acta Apostolicae Sedis,* 101 (2009), no. 26.

is part of culture, and certain religious values are indispensable for a culture to be truly humanising.

The conviction of Pope Benedict XVI that there should be greater co-operation religion and culture, led to his attaching the Pontifical Council for Interreligious Dialogue with the Pontifical Council for Culture on 11 March 2006. He removed the then president of the Pontifical Council for Interreligious Dialogue bishop Michael Fitzgerald, and delegated the direction of the Council to the president of the Pontifical Council for Culture, Cardinal Paul Poupard.[39] This was interpreted by some as devaluing theological dialogue, and an attempt to place dialogue with such religions as Islam, Hinduism, Buddhism, and others, more on the level of culture than on the level of religion. But later, the Vatican decided to make the Pontifical Council for Interreligious Dialogue autonomous again, and have its own president. Consequently, by the end of June 2007 Cardinal Jean-Louis Tauran was appointed as its president of the Council, and he assumed office on 1 September 2007.[40]

Though the decision of Benedict XVI to attach the Pontifical Council for Interreligious Dialogue with the Pontifical Council for Culture, caused some displeasure among certain people in the Church, it pointed to a great truth, namely, that intercultural dialogue cannot be underestimated, and that interreligious dialogue *alone* is not enough to find solutions to the great problems facing the world today.

There are many reasons why *both* interreligious and intercultural of dialogues are important, reasonable and necessary: First, there are religious traditions that are intimately linked to State, politics, social life and culture, and where a separation between religion and State, or religion and politics, or religion and social life, does not exist in the strict sense of the term, or it is not practiced in real life even if such a separation is enshrined in the constitutions of a country. Experience shows that, even if great progress is made in the field of interreligious dialogue, it has very little positive impact on the political, social and

39 Cfr. *L'Osservatore Romano*, 12 marzo 2007, p. 1.

40 Cfr *L'Osservatore Romano*, 25-26 giugno 2007, p. 1.

cultural life of people or nation. What emerges from this experience is that, dialogue with religions cannot be limited only to a theological dialogue; it must also become a dialogue of cultures and civilizations, and this goes beyond the strictly religious sphere and enters into the realm of culture.

Second, there are situations in the world where a State is so fully 'secularised' that, religion has no real influence on the political, social and cultural life of people, and consequently religion and State, or religion and politics never really meet. Consequently, interreligious dialogue has no real impact on the political or social or cultural life of people or on national life. But if there is scope for intercultural dialogue, some of the partners in dialogue can also be religious people, so that some space is provided for an encounter between the 'secular' and the 'religious'.

Third, from a Christian point of view, an exclusively theological dialogue is not possible with non-Christian religions. For example, with non-Christians, one cannot really discuss the doctrine of Trinity, Incarnation, Jesus Christ as Son of God and only Saviour and mediator, etc., which are some of the 'non-negotiables' of Christianity. This means that, many fundamental doctrines and beliefs of Christianity cannot really enter into theological dialogue with the followers of other religions. In the same way, other religions also have their 'non-negotiables' that deal with doctrines and practices, and consequently, the scope of theological dialogue becomes very limited. Besides, real discussions on theology can take place only among a few. But intercultural dialogue is possible between religions where one need not discuss strictly theological issues, and people from different walks of life can participate in it.

Fourth, there are many areas of human life which go beyond the realm of the strictly religious, and enter into the sphere of human values, ethical principles, politics, social life and culture. For example, the defence of ethical values, dignity of human life, fundamental rights, question of co-existence in the concrete terms of politics, economy, history, culture and customs, questions of truth, justice, equality, religious freedom, peace, conflicts, intolerance, violence, terrorism, etc., for which engagement in interreligious dialogue *alone* cannot offer solutions. There should also be serious intercultural dialogue, because many questions lie beyond the sphere of the religious, and enter into the sphere of the human, social, political, economic and cultural life and international relations. Here, dialogue has to be based on the centrality of the human person, and it overrides cultural and ideological contrasts, and includes also people who may not belong to any religion. Hence, the encounter between people has to be a meeting of cultures and religions, and it calls for *both* interreligious and intercultural dialogue. Perhaps this seems to be the new frontier of interreligious relations today.

7. Conclusion

One can neither underestimate the positive results of interreligious dialogue in different parts of the world nor can one be blind to the problems involved in it. Though some express scepticism regarding the usefulness, legitimacy and future of interreligious dialogue, it is here to stay permanently, and it is an irreversible aspect of the mission of the Catholic Church. Perhaps many Catholics are yet to understand the need for it and its advantages for the promotion of the development of individuals and communities, and the positive impact it can have on the world at large, especially to build a world of peace, justice, liberty and brotherhood. The Catholic Church formally opted for interreligious dialogue only in 1965. The Church spread all over the world with its social, cultural, ethnic and linguistic complexities, and the different priorities of the local Churches in their pastoral life, it is too early to expect miracles in interreligious dialogue. Making the lay faithful, pastors and even some major religious leaders convinced of the need for interreligious dialogue, and the formation of people to dialogue will require time because even now ignorance, prejudice, opposition and scepticism about interreligious dialogue are widespread among many Catholics. We are still in the initial stages of interreligious dialogue and the Church needs to make greater efforts in order to give it its rightful place in the mission of the Church. Yet it remains as a fact that, local Churches, parishes, church leaders, educators, educational institutions, catechists, catholic associations, religious congregations, mass media and individual Christians can do a lot more to promote interreligious dialogue.

Conclusion

Interreligious dialogue is integral to the life of the Church, and is one of the main ways in which she reaches out to the followers of other religions. The official documents of the Catholic Church that deal with interreligious dialogue which we have analysed in this study, namely, *Ecclesiam suam* (1964) *Nostra aetate* and other documents of the Vatican II (1962-1965), *Dialogue and Mission* (1984) and *Dialogue and Proclamation* (1991) contain clearly delineated guidelines for dialogue. Obviously these documents must be supplemented by the magisterium of the Popes since the Vatican II, in order to have a more complete and updated vision of the teachings of Church on interreligious dialogue. In addition, one should also study the guidelines of the Pontifical Council for Interreligious Dialogue, the documents issued by the commissions for dialogue in the episcopal conferences, the experience of dialogue at diocesan, regional and national levels, by religious congregations, Pontifical Universities, Catholic dialogue groups, movements and associations, and individual charismatic persons. When these are taken together, they can provide ample proof of the commitment of the Catholic Church to interreligious dialogue, and convince even the hardest sceptic that interreligious dialogue is a living realty in the

Church today, and that it has produced positive results in religious relations.

But the success of interreligious dialogue should not make one ignore the difficulties involved. Some choose to be indifferent to dialogue or place it at the bottom of the pastoral priories of the dioceses, parishes and educational institutions. Interreligious dialogue still remains as an intellectual exercise between experts, often neglecting or side-lining the other legitimate forms of dialogue. The relationship between interreligious dialogue and mission *ad gentes* is another theme that needs further reflection and clarification. The spread of religious fundamentalism remains as a great threat to dialogue. Other obstacles are the denial religious liberty and freedom of conscience to Christians and other religious minorities in certain countries. The complex world of New Religious Movements raises many problems for the Catholics involved in dialogue. The poor selection leaders of dialogue and neglect of their academic training as well as practical experience in dialogue are also problems in dialogue. There is the need to develop a sound theology and spirituality of dialogue, and better acquaintance with the documents of the Church, and the magisterium of the Popes on dialogue by the lay faithful. In this sense, we are still in the initial stages of interreligious dialogue, and so it cannot be expected to have achieved all of the results desired.

The need to promote both interreligious dialogue and intercultural dialogue, and how this can be achieved emerges as a new area for investigation. There is growing interest in interreligious dialogue among statesmen and ambassadors, and this opens up the question of the role of interreligious dialogue in diplomacy. The question of the relationship between interreligious dialogue and religious education, and interreligious dialogue and social communications, are also areas that require close examination.

Education is another important field which should take interreligious dialogue seriously. Some of the potential settings for formal and non-formal dialogue are Catholic schools, colleges, universities, youth centres, youth associations and movements. The dialogue of Christian women with the women of other religions is another area that needs to be explored, especially because in certain cultural settlings men and women do not easily mingle in public.

There is urgent need to make up-to-date the curriculum of religious studies and interreligious dialogue in Pontifical Universities. While some Pontifical Universities offer excellent courses on world religions and interreligious dialogue, others rest content with elementary courses on these subjects. Studies have shown that there are seminaries without a programme for teaching interreligious dialogue.[1] It has also been pointed out that the Congregation for Catholic Education oversees the Church's vast network of seminaries, universities, faculties and schools. Yet since *Nostra aetate*, it has had little to say about the contribution to interreligious dialogue expected of the church's educational institutions.[2] The Pontifical Council for Interreligious Dialogue likewise pay scant attention to fostering interreligious dialogue in universities.[3] All these reflect the poor implementation of the teachings of the Vatican II and the subsequent magisterium of the Church. It can also be interpreted as a sign that many are living out of touch with the religious reality of today. But with Raimon Panikkar we need to affirm emphatically that, interreligious dialogue is today unavoidable, it is a religious imperative, and a historical duty for which we must suitably prepare.[4]

There is a need for a more up-to-date philosophy and theology of dialogue. The Church needs to develop a well-articulated spirituality of dialogue, a better developed theology of religions, and a well-defined theology of culture. If dialogue is an art, style and method with which the Catholic Church carries out her mission in the world today, a new thinking in these areas is indispensable.

---

1 Cfr.http://groups.creighton.edu/sjdialogue/documents/articles/america_miller.html (25.2.2015).

2 Cfr. Ibid.

3 Cfr. Ibid.

4 Cfr. Raimon Panikkar, *The Intrareligious Dialogue*, p. 40.

Finally, the last official document of the Church on interreligious dialogue was published way back in 1991. Hence, it is desirable that she comes out with another document on the topic which will take into consideration the new developments in the theology of religions, spell out more clearly the nature of the spirituality of dialogue, the relationship between religion and culture, and interreligious dialogue and intercultural dialogue. The document should also provide answers to some of the major questions raised by the opponents of interreligious dialogue, and suggest ways to promote dialogue in the problematic contexts of religious fundamentalism, absence of religious liberty, and culture of secularisation.

Appendix

Nostra Aetate
Declaration on the Relation of the Church to Non-Christian Religions

Proclaimed by His Holiness Pope Paul VI on 28 October 1965

1. In this age of ours, when men are drawing more closely together and the bonds of friendship between different peoples are being strengthened the Church examines with greater care the relation which she has to non-Christian religions. Ever aware of her duty to foster unity and charity among individuals, and even among nations, she reflects at the outset on what men have in common and what tends to promote fellowship among them.

All men form but one community. This is so because all stem from the one stock which God created to people the entire earth (cf. Acts 17:26), and also because all share a common destiny, namely God. His providence, evident goodness, and saving designs extend to all men (cf. Wis. 8:1: Acts 14:17: Rom. 2:6 7: I Tim. 2:4) against the day when the elect are gathered together in the holy city which is illumined by the glory of God, and in whose splendor all peoples will walk (cf. Apoc 21:23 ff.).

Men look to their different religions for an answer to the unsolved riddles of human existence. The problems that weigh heavily on the hearts of men are the same today as in the ages past. What is man? What is the meaning and purpose of life? What is upright behavior, and what is sinful? Where does suffering originate, and what end does it serve? How can genuine happiness be found? What happens at death? What is judgment? What reward follows death? And finally, what is the ultimate mystery, beyond human explanation, which embraces our entire existence, from which we take our origin and towards which we tend?

2. Throughout history even to the present day, there is found among different peoples a certain awareness of a hidden power, which lies behind the course of nature and the events of human life At times there is present even a recognition of a supreme being or still more of a Father. This awareness and recognition results in a way of life that is imbued with a deep religious sense. The religions which are found in more advanced civilizations endeavour by way of well-defined concepts and exact language to answer these questions. Thus in Hinduism men explore the divine mystery and express it both in the limitless riches of myth and the accurately defined insights of philosophy. They seek release from the trials of the present life by ascetical practices, profound meditation and recourse to God in confidence and love. Buddhism in its various forms testifies to the essential inadequacy of this changing world. It proposes a way of life by which men can with confidence and trust, attain a state of perfect liberation and reach supreme illumination either through their own efforts or by the aid of divine help. So, too, other religions which are found throughout the world attempt in their own ways to calm the hearts of men by outlining a program of life covering doctrine, moral precepts and sacred rites.

The Catholic Church rejects nothing of what is true and holy in these religions. She has a high regard for the manner of life and conduct, the precepts and doctrines which, although differing in many ways from her own teaching, nevertheless often reflect a ray of that truth which enlightens all men Yet she proclaims and is in duty bound to proclaim without fail, Christ who is the way, the truth and the life (Jn. 1:6). In him, in whom God reconciled all things to himself (2 Cor. 5:18-19), men find the fullness of their religious life.

The Church therefore, urges her sons to enter with prudence and charity into discussion and collaboration with members of other religious. Let Christians, while witnessing to their own faith and way of life, acknowledge, preserve and encourage the spiritual and moral truths found among non-Christians also their social life and culture.

3. The Church has also a high regard for the Muslims. They worship God, who is one, living and subsistent, merciful and almighty, the Creator of heaven and earth,[1] who has also spoken to men. They strive to submit themselves without reserve to the bidden decrees of God, just as Abraham submitted himself to God's plan, to whose faith Muslims eagerly link their own. Although not acknowledging him as God, they worship Jesus as a prophet, his virgin Mother they also honor, and even at times devoutly invoke. Further, they await the day of judgment and the reward of God following the resurrection of the dead. For this reason they highly esteem an upright life and worship God, especially by way of prayer, alms-deeds and fasting.

Over the centuries many quarrels and dissensions have arisen between Christians and Muslims. The sacred Council now pleads with all to forget the past, and urges that a sincere effort be made to achieve mutual understanding; for the benefit of all men, let them together preserve and promote peace, liberty, social justice and moral values.

---

1 Cf. St. Gregory VII, Letter 21 to Anzir (Nacir), King of Mauretana (*PL* 148, col. 450 ff).

4. Sounding the depths of the mystery which is the Church, this sacred Council remembers the spiritual ties which link the people of the New Covenant to the stock of Abraham.

The Church of Christ acknowledges that in God's plan of salvation the beginning of her faith and election is to be found in the patriarchs. Moses and the prophets. She professes that all Christ's faithful, who as men of faith are sons of Abraham (cf. Gal. 3:7), are included in the same patriarch's call and that the salvation of the Church is mystically prefigured in the exodus of God's chosen people from the land of bondage On this account the Church cannot forget that she received the revelation of the Old Testament by way of that people with whom God in his inexpressible mercy established the ancient covenant. Nor can she forget that she draws nourishment from that good olive tree onto which the wild olive branches of the Gentiles have been grafted (cf. Rom. 11:17-24). The Church believes that Christ who is our peace has through his cross reconciled Jews and Gentiles and made them one in himself (cf. Eph. 2:14-16).

Likewise, the Church keeps ever before her mind the words of the apostle Paul about his kinsmen: "they are Israelites, and to them belong the sonship, the glory, the covenants, the giving of the law the worship, and the promises; to them belong the patriarchs, and of their race according to the flesh, is the Christ" (Rom. 9:4-5), the son of the virgin Mary. She is mindful, moreover, that the apostles, the pillars on which the Church stands, are of Jewish descent, as are many of those early disciples who proclaimed the Gospel of Christ to the world.

As holy Scripture testifies, Jerusalem did not recognize God's moment when it came (cf. Lk. 19:42) Jews for the most part did not accept the Gospel; on the contrary, many opposed The spreading of it (cf. Rom. 11:28). Even so, the apostle Paul maintains that the Jews remain very dear to God. for the sake of the patriarchs since God does not take back the gifts he bestowed or the choice he made.[2] Together with the prophets and that same apostle, the Church awaits the day, known to God alone, when all peoples will call on God with

2 Cf. Rom 11:28-29; cf. Dogm. Const. *Lumen Gentium AAS* 57 (1965), 20.

one voice and "serve him shoulder to shoulder" (Soph. 3 :9 cf. Is. 66:23; Ps. 65:4; Rom. 11:11-32)

Since Christians and Jews have such a common spiritual heritage, this sacred Council wishes to encourage and further mutual understanding and appreciation. This can be obtained, especially, by way of biblical and theological enquiry and through friendly discussions.

Even though the Jewish authorities and those who followed their lead pressed for the death of Christ (cf. John 19:6), neither all Jews indiscriminately at that time, nor Jews today, can be charged with the crimes committed during his passion. lt. is true that the Church is the new people of God, yet the Jews should not be spoken of as rejected or accursed as if this followed from holy Scripture. Consequently, all must take care, lest in catechizing or in preaching the Word of God, they teach anything which is not in accord with the truth of the Gospel message or the spirit of Christ.

Indeed the Church reproves every form of persecution against whomsoever it may be directed. Remembering, then, her common heritage with the Jews and moved not by any political consideration, but solely by the religious motivation of Christian charity, she deplores all hatreds, persecutions, displays of antisemitism leveled at any time or from any source against the Jews.

The Church always held and continues to hold that Christ out of infinite love freely underwent suffering and death because of the sins of all men, so that all might attain salvation. It is the duty of the Church, therefore, in her preaching to proclaim the cross of Christ as the sign of God's universal love and the source of all grace.

5. We cannot truly pray to God the Father of all if we treat any people in other than brotherly fashion, for all men are created in God's image. Man's relation to God the Father and man's relation to his. Fellow-men are so dependent on each other that the Scripture says "he who does not love. does not know God" (I Jn. 4:8).

There is no basis therefore, either in theory or in practice for any discrimination between individual and individual, or between people and people arising either from human dignity or from the rights which flow from it.

Therefore, the Church reproves, as foreign to the mind of Christ, any discrimination against people or any harassment of them on the basis of their race, color, condition in life or religion. Accordingly, following, the footsteps of the holy apostles Peter and Paul, the sacred Council earnestly begs the Christian faithful to "conduct themselves well among the Gentiles" (I Pet. 2:12) and if possible, as far as depends on them, to be at peace with all men (cf. Rom 12:18) and in that way to be true sons of the Father who is in heaven (cf. Mt. 5:45).

Source: *Nostra aetate*, Declaration on the Relation of the Church to Non-Christian Religions, in *Vatican Council II. The Conciliar and Post Conciliar Documents*, Austin Flannery (ed.), Bombay, St Paul Publications, 1983, 667-671. [Original text in Latin: *Nostra aetate*, in *Acta Apostolicae Sedis*, 58 (1966), 740-744]

Bibliography

Ad gentes, in *Acta Apostolicae Sedis,* 58 (1966), 947-990.

Apostolicam actuositatem, in *Acta Apostolicae Sedis,* 58 (1966), 837-864.

Arinze Francis, *Meeting Other Believers*, Shillong, Vendrame Institute Publications, 1998.

"L'atteggiamento della Chiesa di fronte ai seguaci di altre religioni. Riflessioni e orientamenti su dialogo e missione", in *Acta Apostolicae Sedis,* 76 (1984), 816-828.

"The Attitude of the Church toward Followers of Other Religions. Reflections and Orientations on Dialogue and Mission, in *Interreligious Dialogue. The Official Teaching of the Catholic Church from the Second Vatican Council to John Paul II (1963-2005),* Francesco Gioia (ed.), Boston, Pauline Books and Media, 2006, 1116-1129.

Augustine, *Le Ritrattazioni*, Testo Latino dell'edizione maurina confrontato con il corpus Christianorum, Ubaldo Pizzani (tr.), Roma, Citta Nuova Editrice, 1994.

Benedict XVI, *Caritas in veritate*, in *Acta Apostolicae Sedis,* 101 (2009), 641-709.

Cassidy Edward Idris, *Ecumenism and Interreligious Dialogue, Unitatis Redintegratio, Nostra Aetate*, New York, Paulist Press, 2005.

Chettimattam John B., "Editorial", *Jeevadhara,* 22 (September 1992), 328-330.

The Christian Faith in the Doctrinal Documents of the Catholic Church, J. Neuner and J. Dupuis (eds.), Bangalore, Theological Publications, 1982.

Christus Dominus, in *Acta Apostolicae Sedis,* 58 (1966), 673-696.

Cleenewerck Laurent, *His Broken Body. Understanding and Healing the Schism between the Roman Catholic and Eastern Orthodox Churches (An Orthodox Perspective),* Washington, Euclid University Consortium Press, 2007.

Clement of Alexandria, *Exhortation to the Heathen* (*Protrepticus*), Philip Schaff *et al* (trs.) Memphis, Bottom of the Hill Publishing, 2012.

________, *Miscellanies (Stromata),* Memphis, Bottom of the Hill Publishing, 2012.

Corneille Catherine, *The Im-Possibility of Interreligious Dialogue*, New York, The Crossroad Publishing Company, 2008.

Danielou Jean, *God and the Ways of Knowing,* Walter Roberts (tr.), San Francisco, Ignatius Press, 1957.

Dei verbum, in *Acta Apostolicae Sedis,* 58 (1966), 817-830.

Dhavamony Mariasusai, "Evangelisation and Dialogue in Vatican II", in *Vatican II Assessment and Perspectives Twenty-five Years after (1962-1987),* Vol. 3, New York, Paulist Press, 1989, 264-281.

Dialogo e Annuncio in *Acta Apostolicae Sedis,* 84 (1992), 414-446.

Dialogo e Missione in *Acta Apostolicae Sedis,* 76 (1984), 816-828.

"Dialogue and Proclamation. Reflection and Orientations on Interreligious Dialogue and the Proclamation of the Gospel of Jesus Christ ", in *Interreligious Dialogue. The Official Teaching of the Catholic Church from the Second Vatican Council to John Paul II (1963-2005),* Francesco Gioia (ed.), Boston, Pauline Books and Media, 2006, 1156-1189.

Dignitatis humanae, in *Acta Apostolicae Sedis,* 58 (1966), 929-941.

Dupuis Jacques, "Interreligious Dialogue in the Church's Evangelizing Mission. Twenty years of Evolution of a Theological Concept", in *Vatican II Assessment and Perspectives Twenty-five Years after (1962-1987),* Vol. 3, New York, Paulist Press, 1989, 237-263.

________, "A Theological Commentary: Dialogue and Proclamation", in William R. Burrows (ed.), *Redemption and Dialogue. Reading Redemptoris Missio and Dialogue and Proclamation*, Oregon, Wipf and Stock Publishers, 1993, 119-158.

________, *Toward a Christian Theology of Religious Pluralism,* New York, Orbis Books, 2001.

________, *Christianity and the Religions. From Confrontation to Dialogue*, Philip Berryman (tr.), New York, Orbis Books, 2002.

Fitzgerald Michael L, "A Theological Reflection on Interreligious Dialogue", in *Catholic Engagement with World Religions. A Comprehensive Study*, Karl Josef Becker and Ilaria Morali (eds.), New York, Orbis Books, 2010, 383-394.

Fitzgerald Michael L. and Borelli John, *Interfaith Dialogue. A Catholic View*, New York, Orbis Books, 2006.

Flannery Austin (ed.), *Vatican Council II. The Conciliar and Post-Conciliar Documents,* Bombay, St. Paul Publications, 1975.

Gaillardetz Richard R. Gaillardetz and Clifford Catherine E. Clifford, *Keys to the Council. Unlocking the Teachings of Vatican II*, Minnesota, Liturgical Press, 2012.

Gaudium et spes, in *Acta Apostolicae Sedis,* 58 (1966), 1025-1115.

Gawron Krystian, *Dialogue in the Teachings of Pope Paul VI*, London, Veritas, 1993.

Granfield P., "Paul VI, Pope", in *New Catholic Encyclopedia*, Vol. 11, Washington, Gale, 2003², 26-33.

Griffiths Paul J., *An Apology for Apologetics. A Study in the Logic of Interreligious Dialogue,* New York, Orbis Books, 1991.

Guitton Jean, *The Pope Speaks. Dialogues of Paul VI with Jean Guitton*, Anne and Christopher Fremantle (tr.), New York, Meredith Press, 1968.

Hahnenberg Edward P., *A Concise Guide to the Documents of Vatican II*, Cincinnati, Franciscan Media, 2007.

Hamilton Lee H., "Foreword", in Douglas Johnston (ed.), *Faith-Based Diplomacy. Trumping Realpolitik*, Oxford, Oxford University Press, 2003, ix-x.

Hebblethwaite, Peter, *Paul VI. The First Modern Pope*, New York, Paulist Press, 1993.

Hedges Paul, *Controversies in Interreligious Dialogue and the Theology of Religions*, London, SCM Press, 2010.

Huber George, *Pilgrim of Peace*, Montreal, Palm Publishers, 1967.

Hussar Bruno, "Genesi storica alla dichiarazione conciliare 'Nostra aetate'", in *La Dichiarazione su "Le Relazioni della Chiesa con le Religioni non Cristiane". Genesi e Storia*, Torino, Elle Di Ci, 1986, 11-46.

Insegnamenti di Benedetto XVI, Vol. I, Vatican City, Libreria Editrice Vaticana, 2006.

Insegnamenti di Benedetto XVI, Vol. III part 2, Vatican City, Libreria Editrice Vaticana, 2008.

Insegnamenti di Benedetto XVI, Vol. V part 1, Vatican City, Libreria Editrice Vaticana, 2010.

Insegnamenti di Benedetto XVI, Vol. VII part 1, Vatican City, Libreria Editrice Vaticana, 2012.

Insegnamenti di Giovanni Paolo II, Vol. VII part 1, Citta del Vaticano, Libreria Editrice Vaticana, 1984.

Insegnamenti di Giovanni Paolo II, Vol. IX part 2, Città del Vaticano, Libreria Editrice Vaticana, 1986.

Insegnamenti di Giovanni Paolo II, Vol. XI part 2, Citta del Vaticano, Libreria Editrice Vaticana, 1989.

Insegnamenti di Giovani Paolo II, Vol. XII part 1, Città del Vaticano, Libreria Editrice Vaticana, 1991.

Insegnamenti di Paolo VI, Vol. II, Città del Vaticano, Tipografia Poliglotta Vaticana, 1964.

Insegnamenti di Paolo VI, Vol. XI, Città del Vaticano, Tipografia Poliglotta Vaticana, 1973.

Insegnamenti di Paolo VI, Vol. XII, Città del Vaticano, Tipografia Poliglotta Vaticana, 1974.

Irenaeus of Lyons, *Aganist Heresies*, The Complete English Translation from the first volume of *The Ante-Nicene Fathers,* Alexander Roberts, James Donaldson, A. Cleveland Coxe (eds.), Marston Gate, Ex Fontibus, new edition, 2010.

Jeevadhara, 22 (September 1992), 328-403.

John Paul II, *Dominem et Vivificatem*, in *Acta Apostolicae Sedis,* 78 (1986), 809-900.

________, *Redemptor Hominis*, in *Acta Apostolicae Sedis,* 71 (1979), 257-324.

________, *Redemptor Hominis*, in *Insegnamenti di Giovanni Paolo II*, Vol. II, Città del Vaticano, Libreria Editrice Vaticana, 1979, 550-609.

________, *Redemptoris Missio*, in *Acta Apostolicae Sedis,* 83 (1991), 249-340.

Johnston Douglas and Sampson Cynthia (eds.), *Religion, the Missing Dimension of Statecraft*, Oxford, Oxford University Press, 1994.

Justin Martyr, *The First Apology*, in *The Fathers of the Church. A New Translation*, Vol. 6, Hermigild Dressler (ed.), *Writings of Saint Justin Martyr*, Thomas B. Falls (tr.), Washington, The Catholic University Press of America, [1948], 2008, 21-111.

________, *The Second Apology*, in *The Fathers of the Church. A New Translation*, Vol. 6, Hermigild Dressler (ed.), *Writings of Saint Justin Martyr*, Thomas B. Falls (tr.), Washington, The Catholic University Press of America, [1948], 2008, 113-135.

Karl Barth: Church Dogmatics. A Selection with Introduction by Helmut Gollwitzer, G.W. Bromiley (tr. and ed.), Edinburgh, T and T Clark, 1961.

Knitter Paul F., *No Other Name? A Critical Survey of Christian Attitudes Towards the World Religions*, London, SCM Press, 1985.

________, *Jesus and Other Names. Christian Mission and Global Responsbility,* New York, Orbis Books, 1996.

________, *Introducing Theologies of Religions*, New York, Maryknoll, 2008.

Kramer Hendrik, *The Christian Message in a Non-Christian World*, New York, Harper, 1938.

Küng Hans, "Foreword to the Second Edition", in Hans Küng, Josef van Ess, Heinich von Stietencron, Heinz Bechert, *Christianity and World Religions. Paths of Dialogue with Islam, Hinduism, and Buddhism,* Peter Heinegg (tr.), New York, Orbis Books, 1993, xi-xiii.

________, *On Being Christian*, Edward Quinn (tr.), London, Xpress Reprints, 1995.

Küster Volker, "Who, With Whom, About What? Exploring the Landscape of Interreligious Dialogue", in *Exchange Journal of Missiological and Ecumenical Research*, 33:1, Brill Academic Publishers, Leiden 2004, 73-92.

Kuttianimattathil Jose, *Practice and Theology of Interreligious Dialogue*, Bangalore, Kristu Jyoti Publications, 1998.

Lotz Johannes B., "Christianity and the Non-Christian Religions in their Relationship to Religious Experience", in *Vatican II Assessment and Perspectives Twenty-five Years after (1962-1987),* Vol. 3, New York, Paulist Press, 1989, 161-183.

Luise Raffaele, *Raimon Panikkar. Profeta del dopodomani*, Milano, San Paolo Edizioni, 2011.

Lumen gentium, in *Acta Apostolicae Sedis,* 57 (1965), 1-67.

Newman John Henry, *An Essay on the Development of Christian Doctrine*, Notre Dame, University of Notre Dame Press, [1878], 6th edition, 1989.

Nostra aetate, in *Acta Apostolicae Sedis,* 58 (1966), 740-744.

Nostra aetate, Declaration on the Relation of the Church to Non-Christian Religions, in *Vatican Council II. The Conciliar and Post Conciliar Documents*, Austin Flannery (ed.), Bombay, St Paul Publications, 1983, 667-671.

O'Malley John W., *What Happened at Vatican II*, Massachusetts, The Belknap Press of Harvard University Press, 2008.

Optatam totius, in *Acta Apostolicae Sedis,* 58 (1966), 713-727.

L'Osservatore Romano, 12 marzo 2007, 1.

L'Osservatore Romano, 25-26 giugno 2007, 1.

Panikkar Raimon, *The Intrareligious Dialogue*, New York, Paulist Press, 1978.

________, *The Unknown Christ of Hinduism. Towards and Ecumenical Christophany*, Bangalore, Asian Trading Corporation, revised and enlarged edition, 1982.

________, *Myth, Faith and Hermeneutics. Cross-Cultural Studies*, Bangalore, Asian Trading Corporation, 1983.

________, *Cultural Disarmament, The Way to Peace,* Robert R. Barr (tr.), Louisville, Westminster John Knox Press, 1995.

Paul VI, *Ecclesiam suam*, in *Acta Apostolicae Sedis,* 56 (1964), 609-659.

________, *Progrediente Concilio*, in *Acta Apostolicae Sedis,* 56 (1964), 560.

________, *Evangelii Nuntiandi*, in *Acta Apostolicae Sedis,* 68 (1976), 1-76.

Pontifical Council for Interreligious Dialogue, *The Official Teachings of the Catholic Church from the Second Vatican Council to John Paul II (1963-2005*), Francesco Gioia (ed.), Boston, Pauline Books and Media, 2006.

Pontificio Consiglio per il Dialogo Interreligioso e Congregazione per l'Evangelizzazione dei Popoli, "Dialogo e annuncio: Riflessioni e orientamenti sull'annuncio del vangelo e il dialogo interreligioso", in *Enchiridion Vaticanum. Documenti Ufficiali della Santa Sede 1991-1993*, Vol. 13, Testo ufficiale e versione Italiana, Bologna, Centro Editoriale Dehoniano, 1995, 191-229.

Rahner Karl und Vorgrimler Herbert, *Kleines Konzilskompendium*, Freiburg, Herder, 1966.

Rahner Karl, *Theological Investigations*, Vol. 10. *Writings of 1965-1967 (2*), David Bourke (tr.), London, Darton, Longman and Todd, 1973.

Rudolf Heredia, "Religious Fundamentalism: Reaction and Response", *Vidyajyoti,* 68, January, 2004, 30-43.

Sacrosanctum concilium, in *Acta Apostolicae Sedis,* 56 (1964), 97-134.

Segretariato per i Non-Cristiani, "L'atteggiamento della Chiesa di fronte ai seguaci di altre religioni. Riflessioni e orientamenti su dialogo e missione", in *Enchiridion Vaticanum. Documenti Ufficiali della Santa Sede 1983-1985,* Vol. 9, Testo ufficiale e versione Italiana, Bologna, Centro Editoriale Dehoniano, 1987, 928-943.

Sharpe Erich J., "Dialogue of Religions", in Mircea Eliade (ed.), *Encyclopedia of Religion,* Vol. 4, New York, Macmillan Company, 1987, 344-348.

Smith Jane Idleman, *Muslims, Christians, and the Challenge of Interfaith Dialogue*, Oxford, Oxford University Press, 2007.

Thuruthiyil Scaria, *Principi e valori educativi nella tradizione Indiana*, Roma, Edizioni Progetto Cultura, 2010.

Tauran Jean Louis, "Rendere ragione della propria speranza", in *Il dialogo interreligioso come fondamento della civiltà*, Enrico Bertoni (a cura di), Milano, Maretti, 2009, 73-79.

Wilfred Felix, "Dialogue Gasping for Breath? Towards New Frontiers in Interreligious Dialogue, *Vidyajyoti,* 51 (October 1987), 449-466.

Zago Marcello, *Buddhismo e Cristianesimo in Dialogo. Situazione, Rapporti, Convergenze*, Roma, Citta Nuova Editrice, 1985.

________, *La Nostra aetate e il Dialogo Interreligioso a ventanni dal Concilio*, Monferrato, Edizioni Piemme, 1986.

Website materials

http://en.wikipedia.org/wiki/Irenicism (14.10.2014).

http://en.wikipedia.org/wiki/Pontifical_Council_for_Interreligious_Dialogue (24.3.2015).

http://groups.creighton.edu/sjdialogue/documents/articles/america_miller.html (25.2.2015).

http://tomryancsp.org/proclamation.htm (22.1.2014).

http://www.cimer.org.au/documents/DialogueandMission1984.pdf (3.2.2014).

http://www.vatican.va/holy_father/paul_vi/encyclicals/documents/hf_p-vi_enc_06081964_ecclesiam_en.html (14.2. 2015).

http://www.vatican.va/roman_curia/pontifical_councils/chrstuni/documents/rc_pc_chrstuni_pro_20051996_chrstuni_pro_en.html (9.10. 2014).

http://www.vatican.va/roman_curia/pontifical_councils/interelg/documents/rc_pc_interelg_pro_20051996_en.html (23.2.2015).

Index

E

F

T

U

W